What Others Are Saying A**

"Imagine if Indiana Jones had died young leaving a teenage daughter somewhat disenfranchised and vaguely aware of his adventures. Then, fifty years later a box of his things filled with clues and a recording from a friend of her father's sets her on an adventure across the globe to discover the truth about her father's past. This is *Landing in My Present* and the most amazing thing is it is all true! Mary Clark's attention to detail allows you to easily slip into a long gone era without letting the details get in the way of her fast-paced telling of this fascinating World War II story. Her father's adventures seemingly touch on every continent while centered on his perilous flights from India across the Himalayas to resupply the Chinese, a perilous route known as 'The Hump.' It's part mystery thriller, part history class, part travelogue, and 100% page burning awesomeness!"

—*Jeffrey Lehmann, host and producer of the multi Emmy award-winning* Weekend Explorer *travel series on PBS and broadcasters worldwide*

"A true account of a fantastic quest to know a father, a WWII veteran originally from the Texas Panhandle. Like many war veterans, he kept his experience to himself. Mary Clark reveals a growing understanding of the father she'd always wished to know. Since he died when she was sixteen, she'd retained only a teen-aged memory of him and a strong desire to know about his adult life. She gives us step by step evidence—by traveling to remotes parts of his world—of her father's service providing supplies from India to American allies in China. Letters from his friends, and memories from other pilots reveal a quiet hero. 'Flying the Hump,' he endured icy frigid skies 150 times while carrying mostly gasoline and little hope of rescue if he failed. Readers will appreciate Clark's careful investigation and her exemplary style while writing about an emotional journey of discovery."

—*Carolyn Osborn, author of* Durations: A Memoir and Personal Essays; *recipient of the Lon Tinkle Lifetime Achievement Award from the Texas Institute of Letters*

"Mary Clark's odyssey of a woman's rediscovery of her father intertwines two compelling stories, her search for a parent who died tragically young, and whom she never really knew, and the shattering realization of her own buried grief as she sets out to learn who he was. She takes a deeply honest look back at the hard-working family who could not bring themselves to voice what she calls 'the unanswered questions that should have been asked.' She unearths unexpected treasure in rare, precious accounts of those who knew him. A moving journey leads her to the other side of the world, where he served as a pilot flying the forbidding Himalayas in the perilous Hump Airlift of World War II. Beautifully remembered, Mary Clark shares her wonder as the 'grainy black and white' picture of her father comes into focus, in this story of a daughter's quest and a daughter's love, and the heroic but endearingly human man she finds."

—*Nedda R. Thomas, author of* Hump Pilot: Defying Death Flying the Himalayas in World War II

"Reading Mary Clark's description of Flying the Hump in *Landing in My Present* brought back many memories. I really don't know how she was able to capture so well the details of her father's experiences flying in India and China." —*Stuart Arnold, former Australian Hump Pilot and retired pilot for Trans-Australian Airlines*

"The pilots that flew the Hump made a huge contribution to China's defense against the Japanese invasion. This history is well known in China and we are grateful to the pilots who helped us. I am happy that Mary Clark wrote about this important story." —*Xiaomei Wu, Chinese citizen*

"*Landing in My Present* is a touching daughter's love letter to her father. Through letters and stories discovered fifty years after his death at a young age, the author 'meets' him through the eyes of an adult. World War II fans will appreciate the stories of his years as a pilot in the Army Air Force flying dangerous transport missions from India to China."

—*Katrina Shawver, author of* Henry: A Polish Swimmer's True Story of Friendship from Auschwitz to America.

LANDING IN MY PRESENT

Published by Hellgate Press
(An imprint of L&R Publishing, LLC)
PO Box 3531
Ashland, OR 97520
email: info@hellgatepress.com

Interior Design: L. Redding
Cover Design: Angelia Herndon and Tom Herndon, Jr.
Cover Photo: David W. Cook.
ISBN: 978-1-55571-985-2

Printed and bound in the United States of America
First edition 10 9 8 7 6 5 4 3 2 1

To my flying father who was more present than I ever imagined and to those who contributed the pieces to make his spirit come to life.

Contents

LANDING IN MY PRESENT

A Father, a Daughter, and the Singular
Himalayan Journey that Reunited Them

MARY WALKER CLARK

7/12/2022

To Dennis Noblett, who will recognize much about the Walker family. Perry's father was my uncle and my father's partner in the produce business. I hope you enjoy the story. All the best, Mary W Clark

Hellgate Press   Ashland, Oregon

The Mont Jennings Tape

June 2000

 "I have something for you," Aunt Helen calls out as she hurries to my side, quickly grabbing my arm and steering me away from the throng of relatives at a rare Walker family reunion. Without any of her usual greetings or hugs, Helen continues: "I've interviewed a man who flew with your father in World War II," she explains, thrusting a microcassette into my hand. "Here's his story. You have to listen to it."

 When I did, it changed my life.

 Before his death I hardly knew my father. I was sixteen when he died and our relationship until then was superficial, lacking the maturity added age could have provided. He was often absent. He never talked about his war days…or much about his life at all. He certainly never talked about his extraordinary experiences flying the Hump, a treacherous series of US missions that transported supplies over the Himalayas to China in the 1940s.

 Aunt Helen recognized the importance of this find for two reasons. As a retired librarian, she knew how rare it was to find information on my father's war days. She was also sensitive to the void in my life from the early loss of my father.

 It would take fourteen years before I could begin to experience the full impact on my life of that tiny Dictaphone tape. By then I was retired from my law practice and our children were grown. I finally had the

freedom to let Aunt Helen's gift launch a journey for me that was nearly
as incredible in its own way as my dad's had been for him. In the end,
it gave me back my father.

* * *

MY FATHER'S BEST friend was on the battleship Utah the day
Pearl Harbor was attacked. In the years that followed, Lee never
missed an opportunity to describe the horror of his experiences or to re-
unite with fellow survivors. Other veterans spoke of World War II only
with close friends and family, often at the end of their lives. When my husband's father was dying of lung cancer, he opened up for the first time
about being a physician in Europe as the Allies moved north to Germany.
Still, most vets allowed the memories to remain submerged as the challenges of rebuilding the world filled their days.

My father was comfortable in the latter category. He returned to his
hometown to marry, have children, start numerous businesses and blend
into postwar prosperity. He had enough new distractions without needing
to dwell on the past.

I was aware of some of Dad's war history when I launched my journey,
but not much. My mother had kept two important documents: his draft
card and his discharge summary that listed the dates he joined and left the
army and mentioned that he had served abroad for fourteen months.
Some years earlier, my brother Morey had tried to get our father's army
records only to receive a disheartening reply that they had been destroyed
in a fire, closing off an obvious source of Dad's history. What I did know
starting out was that after joining the Army, he became a transport pilot
in the Army Air Force, bringing in troops and supplies where needed.
That included flying the Hump from India over the Himalayas to China,
carrying primarily gasoline to Chinese and American troops. I knew this
to have been a challenging and dangerous mission and that the men who
carried it out should have been proud.

Yet so many questions remained: Where had Dad been stationed during
that time? What had his life been like in those postings? How had he han-
dled the pressure of life-threatening storms over the Himalayas? Had his
experiences affected his role as a father? I had no answers to those first
questions. As for the last one, I didn't sense that he had been traumatized

by his war years when I was growing up. But how could I know? He never brought it up and neither did I, nor did the rest of my family.

After that June 2000 family reunion, I returned home to Paris, Texas, and transcribed Aunt Helen's tape. The pilot she'd interviewed, the one who had flown with my father over the Hump, was Mont Jennings, who lived across the state in Lubbock, as did Aunt Helen.

As I typed Jennings' words, my father's world in India and China began to come into focus. Even though Jennings had only one personal encounter with Dad, on his last flight over the Hump, they'd shared a base location at Misamari, in the Assam Valley of India. Before the tape, all I knew was that Dad had been "somewhere" in India. With Jennings' words, a picture of my father's war life emerged, with details of living conditions, weather challenges, routes, hazards of gunfire below and turnaround time in China. The grainy black-and-white picture I'd had of Dad's military life began to shift into color with Jennings' stories of flying the Hump. I learned where Dad trained, how he crossed the Atlantic, what planes he flew. The background sharpened as the challenges of landing in China became apparent. At times as I typed, I held my breath with childlike anticipation of the next story or detail. Each revelation brought Dad's past into my present world, erasing years of silence. When the tape ended, I sat quietly, disappointed at the brief glimpse it had given me into his war life, longing for more. Yet I felt a connection to Dad that I had never felt before. His war experience had become accessible, tangible for the first time.

Despite my best intentions, however, I couldn't find time in the next decade and a half to pursue more information about Dad and his military life. My days filled with an active law practice, community involvement and children in high school and college. But the Mont Jennings' interview had created a movie reel of war life in India and China that never stopped playing in my mind, always ending too soon, as though the film had snapped mid-story.

In June 2014, when I had retired and life's pace had abated, I could finally review the Jennings transcript. As I did, two locations beckoned with their foreign names — Misamari, India and Kunming, China: the first, where Dad had been based, and the second, the destination for his air missions. They were real places with real people who still lived there. My Dad had lived there once. Suddenly, I wanted to know more and felt drawn to make a journey halfway around the world to go where he had gone and where he had flown. My husband, my oldest brother, Mack, and his wife, Jan, agreed to join me on the family pilgrimage.

As plans for the trip progressed, I expanded my search. And I began by reversing the unspoken decision my family made to bury Dad's memories in our unconscious after his death, a silence that had lasted fifty years. I started by reaching out for the first time to an aunt, cousins and my brothers for family stories. Friends helped me remember childhood experiences. I studied old family photos. Research on the Hump operation added needed information that helped me understand and appreciate my father's war experience. And I slowly looked inward for my memories of Dad, realizing that I was a sixty-six-year-old woman who still saw her father through the eyes of a sixteen-year-old.

This became more than a journey to reconstruct Dad's war experience. I sought a means to enlarge my view of him, learn more about how his past contributed to his success, analyze his approach to parenting from my now experienced viewpoint as a mother, appreciate his business acumen from years of working, observe his community involvement and dedication as a husband, and to question his persistent absences and guarded past. I wanted a mature view of him to replace the stunted one formed decades earlier from his premature death and in a more innocent time.

But how do you broaden your relationship with someone who has been dead for fifty years? First, I had to face the past, and the Mont Jennings interview provided the initial step into my father's undiscovered world and mysterious war days.

LOOKING BACK—1917-1966

ONE

Ray Charles Walker
Date of Death:
November 8, 1966

It is after noon, in my fourth-period physics class. I'm in junior year and have just finished an exam when a student from the central office arrives and quietly asks Mr. Dodd to release me. After gathering my books, I follow her downstairs to the principal's office. I know what has happened and I dread the news.

The small office is filled. Our minister, Rev. Mock, is there in his clerical collar, looking serious. Next to him is my older brother, Mack, and the German exchange student who is living with us, Helmut Gabauer. Mock solemnly delivers the news—my father has died—and then holds me close. Consistent with my controlled nature, I don't burst into tears. I don't ask questions. I don't make eye contact with anyone.

For weeks, since the accident in early October, I have feared this moment. But now I can only wonder if he died when I was in my history class or while I was eating lunch. Was I laughing with friends when he breathed his last? What was I doing when I lost my father?

We wait quietly until my younger brother, Gary, arrives and quickly surveys the sad faces. I tune out the minister's repetition of the same painful news. None of us talks. Only the tenderhearted Gary cries.

Photo of my father, Ray Charles Walker, as used
for his obituary, 1966.

* * *

THE ACCIDENT HAPPENED October 5, 1966, in the middle of
harvesting month for carrots at Walker Brothers Produce Shed. This
time of the fall was the culmination of a year of planning, planting, weed-
ing, fertilizing, watering and, now, bringing to the surface the mature produce. That morning Dad would have cooked his usual bacon and eggs,
probably wondering how to fit everything into his schedule for the day.

Summer and Fall and were busy times for my father. Truckloads of
freshly dug potatoes, carrots and onions with clumps of dirt still clinging
to them were brought to the shed for cleaning and bagging; In the summer
it was "running potatoes," as we called the process. Onions were also
sorted. Carrots arrived later. Freight railcars waited on the other side of
the warehouse for the finished product to be shipped. Dad was an early
promoter of growing vegetables in the Texas Panhandle and he was affectionately known around town as Potato Man. With the nearest produce

shed sixty-five miles away, Dad and his brother, Preston, had started the Walker Brothers company to fill that gap.

Inside the shed, large conveyor belts would carry potatoes, onions and carrots through a sorting process, clanging loudly as the produce moved from one level to the next. Lines of Hispanic men and women picked out blighted vegetables, tossing them into another bin. If one tuned out the conveyor belts, a slight hum of Spanish being spoken could be heard. Dad loved this energy, the result of years of growing the business. My brothers and I knew not to get close to the machines, but I always enjoyed watching the scene play out, smelling the freshly washed produce, wondering where each would land. The US Army bought our potatoes and onions. And Walker Brothers had a contract with Campbell Soup, Frito Lay and other large companies for our produce. I liked thinking of our potatoes or carrots being in those soup cans, distributed around the country.

On that October day, Dad had been at the shed since morning but returned home for dinner with the family. Because of the perishable nature of produce, the cleaning process would continue into the night and Dad left after eating to supervise the evening shift. An hour later Mom got a call. I knew something was wrong from the anxiety in her voice and the quick questions she asked: "When?" "What happened again?" "Where is he?" As soon as she hung up, she turned to us: "Dad collapsed at work and is being taken to the hospital. We've got to go."

Mom called a friend to watch my younger siblings and instructed my older brother, Mack, and me to accompany her, even asking Mack to drive, an indication of her nervousness and concern about her ability to concentrate. At the hospital my brother and I remained in the waiting room while Mom disappeared behind swinging doors into an unfamiliar medical world. Mack and I were old enough to join her, but she wasn't sure of Dad's condition and she chose to leave us behind.

Mack and I waited quietly. It was past visiting hours, the waiting room already empty. We knew little of what had happened other than that a piece of machinery had hit Dad in the head as he was repairing a part. But this had happened during the afternoon, and it wasn't clear whether his later collapse was related. The office manager said Dad complained about a blinding headache just before he collapsed. There was also talk of a stroke. It was confusing. After all, he had seemed fine at dinner.

I wanted to cry but couldn't. Even back then, two of my brothers and I were stoic. No wailing or whimpering for us. It wasn't because of any belittling by our parents; they never told us to shape up or to stop crying. It's just that we refused to reveal our feelings to the outside world. It was somehow innate. Because my fallback was silence, I said nothing. Yet my stomach churned, my heart raced and my mind filled with questions. The situation was so disorienting. Even the clock on the waiting room wall seemed to slow down. I tried to concentrate on the lone telephone operator answering calls from her nearby open office. But all I wanted was for Mom to come out and explain it all.

Within the hour my mother's cousin, Bob Horne, emerged with the news that Dad was being taken by ambulance to a larger hospital in Lubbock, forty-five minutes away. He had not regained consciousness and needed more advanced care than our local hospital could provide. Mom would go with him and we were to return home. Bob acknowledged that Dad's condition was serious but he gave no details. He said only that our father was getting good care and tried to smile encouragingly. I didn't know what to think.

I can't remember who stayed with us that night, but someone did and whoever it was must have helped with breakfast the next morning. We were to go to school, keeping life as normal as possible. But how could it be? In a small Texas town like Plainview, many calls would have been made through the night and early morning, spreading word of the incident. That was clear when I walked into my first class: I was immediately surrounded by friends who already knew of Dad's hospitalization. For some reason, I made light of the situation, trying to convince myself that Dad was going to be all right. I told my friends and teachers he was improving. I said the doctors were encouraging. I said we were hopeful. None of that was true and I knew it as I said it. I just couldn't admit the possibility of anything else.

Over the next five weeks, Dad remained in intensive care in a coma with a bleed in his brain. Today, surgery could be an option to stop the bleeding but that advanced technique was not available in 1966. Our only hope was for the bleed to stop on its own and for Dad to wake up.

For the first days after the call, Mom was in Lubbock most of the time during the day, with many friends and family visiting. Dad wasn't progressing, remaining in a coma. During the week, my routine continued: band and twirling practices, football games, physics experiments, English essays, getting Cokes with girlfriends, listening to the Beatles. Thoughts of my Dad were always close…but not too close. I could feel the fear of his potential death hovering over my everyday life, a shadow at the edge of my consciousness. Gratefully, school provided an important distraction.

After those initial hectic days, Mack would drive my three other brothers and me to Lubbock on weekends. Sometimes, we stayed overnight in a hotel but mostly we just remained for part of a day. Even so, we weren't allowed into the intensive care unit. Instead, we acted as a greeting committee, talking with whomever had come in from Plainview to visit. Part of me wanted to see where Dad was being cared for, but the side that feared seeing him in a diminished capacity was happy to be barred from the ICU.

Surprisingly, Mom didn't try to prepare us for a bad outcome. She saw life in a positive way and was probably concentrating on a hopeful result, at least most of the time. I remember one night at a hotel, though, when my uncle and aunt were visiting. It was just the four of us. I was lying in bed, ready to go to sleep. Mom broke down and cried with a force I had never heard from her, her strangled voice moaning, "He's going to die. He's going to die." My uncle comforted her and I turned to face the wall, allowing some tears to fall, but not wanting to believe her words.

On a visit later that fall, Mom decided Mack, Gary and I needed to see Dad, despite the visiting restrictions. Inside the ICU Dad lay asleep in a bed next to other seriously ill patients, a mask over his mouth, the quiet ventilator pumping life-supporting air into his lungs. The subdued lighting of the unit contributed to a feeling of claustrophobia and I was having trouble breathing, as if experiencing Dad's need for oxygen in a personal way. My father had lost much weight and was hardly recognizable. I recoiled. That person couldn't be my father. I felt I was in the wrong place. I felt like an intruder, staring, and soon looked away. I knew Dad wouldn't want me to see him like this. None of us wanted to stay long and we didn't. Walking out of the hospital, I realized with certainty for the first time that Dad wasn't going to recover. All I wanted to do was run but I didn't. I never saw my father again.

On the evening of November 7, five weeks after the accident, Mom told my brothers and me that Dad was being transferred back to our local hospital. He had never regained consciousness and my mother wanted him closer. At breakfast the following morning, Mom seemed distant and distracted but didn't reveal any inner worries or concerns. She simply said it was time to move Dad. Intuitively, I knew something was serious about this change but was afraid to ask. Our local hospital wasn't as advanced as the one in Lubbock. Dad was still in a coma. Why was she bringing him home? It was years later before I realized she must have known she was bringing him home to die but chose not to share that with her children. With maturity, I admired her for making that decision and deeply felt the sadness and anxiety that would have accompanied the choice she didn't want to make. I wished we had talked during that emotional time but we didn't, an early indication of my family's tilt toward silence, choosing to let traumatic events sink below consciousness.

Other than the fact that Mom's mind was elsewhere, it was an ordinary morning. Marching band practice had ended for the semester, so there was no reason for me to leave early, and the completed homework from my heavy class load was already tucked into my textbooks. Not unusually, I had to rush Gary, our dawdler, to finish eating so that he, Mack, Helmut and I wouldn't be late for school. With Mack driving, we left in the "children's car," a small British Anglia that Dad had brought home for us one day to our surprise and delight, and that was just big enough to hold four teenagers and our books. Mom left to take my younger two brothers to the elementary school and junior high school. It was all so normal until that fourth-period physics class.

After Rev. Mock delivered the news of Dad's death, the principal thoughtfully let us stay in the office until classes changed. After the bell rang, our somber band walked down the empty hall toward the parking lot. My English teacher had just stepped outside a classroom to pin up her attendance sheet. When she saw us, she instinctively knew what must have happened. Everyone on staff was aware of Dad's condition. She caught me in her arms, asking quietly if Dad had died. I could only nod. She said she was sorry and hugged me for a long time, an early indication of what I was soon to face: friends who wanted to be sympathetic and consoling.

When we got home, Mom hurried out of the kitchen, her face stricken, her voice choked with tears. She hugged us individually and was visibly relieved to have her children home. Friends and family members had already begun to arrive, some with food. All I could do was run to my room and shut the door where it was quiet, where I wouldn't have to confront so many grim faces. I closeted myself there, listening to music, trying to soften the knot in my chest, hoping no one would knock. I didn't know what to say to anyone or how to accept sympathy. I don't remember how I got through the rest of the day. I can't remember talking to anyone, eating dinner or sleeping. All these years later, it is still a painful blur.

The funeral was large, at least by small-town standards. As we approached the church in the funeral home limousine, the streets jammed with cars and pickup trucks, I noted with surprise and then a quiet pride the size of the crowd, which overflowed onto the church grounds. As an older friend of mine says, "If you want a large funeral, die young," an observation that always takes me back to Dad's funeral. Hundreds had come to express their condolences, with the large numbers reflecting our family's involvement in the community. My father was in the prime of his life with business contacts across the state. Mom sat on the school board and stayed active in her children's activities. They had friends and family in the area from childhood on, and we five children were just as involved in school activities and busy social lives. There was also a large contingent from school, including my closest friends. The high school had set out clipboards in the office to make it easy for students and teachers to sign out for the funeral. In fact, the crowd was so large that our small Episcopal church had set up overflow seating in the parish hall with speakers to broadcast the service. Even with that, we passed many mourners waiting outside the church as we entered. Numerous Hispanic men stood slightly apart and behind the crowd, hats in hands, faces cast down, some with wives at their side.

Before we left for the funeral, Mom had come into my room and found me staring at my closet. I told her I didn't know what to wear. I had never been to a funeral. She helped me pick out an appropriate dress and suggested I wear my nice coat. Her calm presence helped settle me and let me feel detached from the anxiety in my heart, which allowed me to do little but go through motions that day—from riding in the limousine to walking down the church aisle with every seat filled except the two rows in front reserved for the family to sitting through an unfamiliar service to standing at the gravesite. Years later, a friend of my mother's told me that watching Mom leave the church after the funeral with her five young children trailing behind was the saddest thing she had ever seen, a picture she never could shake. Tears fill my eyes as I write this, tears that should have been shed at the funeral but weren't, even as the men and women around me that day were crying.

When Dad died no book had yet been written about the five stages of grief. No counselor from school approached me or my brothers to check on us. While visibly sympathetic, our Episcopal priest couldn't find the words to comfort us. My mother was mature and emotional enough to suffer through the anger, depression and acceptance. She had probably tried the bargaining component when Dad was in the hospital. The rest of us simply denied. We didn't deny his death. We denied its effect on us. And I denied it for fifty years, until the journey that led to this book. My cousin Carolyn calls this "stuffing." You stuff all the bad news down deep and don't allow it to surface. A more proper description is that we lived in a culture of silent grief. Only in the 1970s did expressive grief and grief counseling get their starts.

When I had to talk of my father to strangers or new friends, I could do it in a calm voice, describing his death and the family he had left behind. For the first years, teachers and friends of my parents would give me extra hugs and that "I am so sorry" look. In my maturity I now understand their need to reach out, but as a teenager and young adult, I wanted them to look away.

I was grateful to my friends for not mentioning it. Our self-centered teenage life continued, even on the day of the funeral. When my best friends came by that evening, my mother let me go to the drive-in movies with them. She didn't want me out in public that day, but she intuitively knew I needed a break from the gloom of the house. A drive-in movie provided the cover.

With Dad's death I knew my life had shifted irrevocably, throwing me off balance and into a world untethered. But at age sixteen, my future vision was short-term, based primarily on high school and college. It was only as each major life event happened without my father that the loss painfully reappeared, as a sharp stab of absence.

For years, anger, the second stage of grief, showed up as envy. There were moments of jealousy and resentment of friends and family with fathers: having a gray-haired father to walk them down the aisle at their weddings while my brother Mack accompanied me, seeing cousins inherit large estates, the results of a full working lifetime, not one truncated by death. Even watching my husband, Ed, drive to Austin for weeks before his father's death to talk and finally hear his war stories made me happy for him, but frustrating for me.

I didn't express these feelings, choosing to ignore them or to look on the bright side of a situation. Mack looked snazzy in his white suit and long hair at my wedding as we walked down the aisle together. Education was the substitute for an inheritance in my family when it came to increased earning capacity. And I didn't have to watch Dad grow old. Because of his early death, he never aged. His skin stayed smooth, his shoulders remained erect and his back was always straight. The energy needed to fuel his work as a farmer and successful businessman, such as starting a field of irrigation pipes, driving a tractor, supervising his growing number of businesses and helping, even tangentially, raise a family never diminished. Dad never grayed, and his knees didn't cripple with arthritis. His eyes never clouded with cataracts. We never had to discuss the need to move him out of the family home nor take away his driving privileges. While my mother diminished in stature, lost firmness in her skin and details of her memory, my father perpetually smiled back at me in the prime of his life.

But the optimistic approach was never enough of a facade to completely mask the absence. Dad wasn't there when I graduated high school. He never visited me in college. My children were without a grandfather. My mother's financial support was more limited. We never had an adult conversation that allowed us to relate on a more mature level, with respect for the other's intellect and beliefs. It all added up to a sizable loss, one that revealed itself unceasingly as I matured.

What I didn't see until later was the biggest loss of all: his story. I couldn't ask him about his growing up on a farm, why he chose Mom to marry, how he started his own business, what his spiritual beliefs were or even what inspired him to fly. The questions are endless today, but I was blind to them for years.

Somehow, my World War II and personal quests took me first to the memories of those two autumn days in 1966, both of which dawned beautifully. The events of only two dates in my teenage life prematurely taught me certain adult lessons about the fragility of life and how quickly it can all change, a lesson my father would have been painfully familiar with from his World War II experiences. Dad had faced countless dangers in the war, surviving when many didn't. He was saved by his knowledge of flying but also by the machines that carried him. In the end, ironically, it was a mechanical accident that felled him, far from the Himalayas and his war days. His plane finally went down, if only metaphorically, a peace-time casualty…and I became a civilian next of kin.

TWO

A Trunk in the Attic

"Dad had a trunk from World War II," my brother Gary casually notes at breakfast as my husband and I talk of our planned trip to India and China.

"Dad had a trunk from World War II!?"

"Yes, he did," Gary smiles, enjoying my astonishment.

"Where is it?"

"In the attic," he replies, still smiling.

"In your attic, as in upstairs?" I sputter. "What's in it?"

"Oh, letters from his pilot students, pictures, his flying jacket... memorabilia from the war."

I can only stare with my mouth open, trying to grasp the potential of this discovery.

"I'll go get it," Gary offers.

Gary brings a pine-planked trunk down from his attic and dramatically drops it in the middle of the kitchen table. On the outside, in large bold lettering, is my grandfather's name, R.E. Walker and his address in Plainview. Gary opens the box. I look up, smile broadly at the family circle and rub my hands together in anticipation.

* * *

Address on my father's WWII trunk sent from Africa.

A TRUNK HIDDEN away in Gary's attic. Really? It was February 2016 and my husband and I were at Gary's home in Albuquerque, discussing plans for the Asia trip. Gary and his wife, Karen, weren't coming but were interested in the details.

Preparations for our trip had progressed: We had a departure a date in November, a month after the monsoon rains would have ended but before cold weather could intrude, and we had tickets from Emirates Airlines, a company that would have surprised my father by its location. When Dad had traveled through the Middle East, Dubai was a dusty trading seaport known for pearls and fish, far from the aeronautic center it has become.

All seemed on course for the journey that day at Gary and Karen's, except for one thing: After I booked our tickets but before we got to my brother's, I reread my transcript of the Mont Jennings interview and had an unexpected concern that we were going to the wrong place!

Because of what I had remembered of the Jennings interview, Misamari was to be our primary destination in India. I now knew about the geography of the Assam Valley and its dominant Brahmaputra River, located just a few miles south of Misamari. I loved saying "the Brahmaputra," spouting it out with authority as I talked of our trip's itinerary with friends. My Indian friends would nod in recognition of the river's name and significance. It is one of the major rivers of Asia, fourteen hundred miles long, originating in Tibet and flowing through the Assam Valley and into the delta of Bangladesh. The river continues to reshape the valley with yearly floods. It played a prominent role for the World War II Hump pilots, as they used it to help orient themselves after takeoff and before landing. We would be crossing it more than once on our journey.

Unfortunately, the transcript, once I reread it, didn't refer to the Brahmaputra. It referred to the Ganges, which was nowhere near Misamari. Had I made a colossal blunder in planning the trip? Were we going to the wrong place? Jennings' details on his time in India were so specific that I couldn't imagine he had the wrong name for the river. At the same time, I remember struggling to understand Jennings when he talked about the river. Had I simply typed "Ganges" because it was the only river in India I then knew?

Sitting at my brother's breakfast table that morning, I bemoaned this turn of events and expressed my anxiety at the discovery. The Assam Valley was the historical place for the launching of the Hump operation and included Misamari, but there were also bases in other parts of India. The Ganges River would have been hundreds of miles further away from China. Either Jennings misremembered the name of the river, I typed it wrong or we needed to start over. Did I dare hope that the answer would be tucked away in the newly discovered trunk?

Gary's revelation of the existence of Dad's trunk was both exciting and disturbing. Why had I not known about it? Gary wouldn't have hidden the information. In fact, he had probably told us that he was taking it when we moved Mom from her big family home to a retirement center. He may have even indicated what was inside. Whatever he told us, I didn't hear it. Not really. It hadn't mattered to me back then. Now, with the planned trip to India and China, it mattered a lot.

The return address in big letters on the trunk was an APO (Army Post Office) address out of Miami, Florida. Although I had seen them on letters for years, APOs had long been a mystery to me, not understanding exactly how those numbers directed the mail. Later in my journey, a friend alerted me to a site that listed World War II APOs. It proved to be key in tracking Dad. From the site I learned that my father had been in Maiduguri, Nigeria when he sent the box home. Weathered American stamps revealed the shipping cost from Africa to Texas: $3.11.

Inside the trunk, dozens of letters from former students were addressed to Dad in Uvalde, Texas, where he taught beginning pilots to fly at the start of the war. A couple of wedding announcements and some pilot graduation invitations indicated Dad's importance to people I had never heard of. Christmas cards reflected his location for the holidays over the years. And a love poem from a Margie in Wichita, Kansas raised all kinds of questions and revealed an emotional side of Dad that I didn't feel right about reading but would eventually.

There was more. Two menus from locations inside Africa confirmed Dad had spent Thanksgiving 1944 in the Gold Coast (now Ghana) and Christmas that year somewhere in Africa. Dad had saved the program from the Protestant Christmas Eve service that included a choir and carols. Raised a Baptist, he would have been more comfortable with this blend of Protestant traditions than with the Catholic service. I couldn't know what he was praying for or whether he was lonely and missing home. But just knowing where he was and when was enough, more than enough. My father spent Christmas Eve in Africa. The sound of that was so mysterious, so different from the many war stories out of Europe. He heard the Christmas story read near actual camels as he looked out on a foreign sky with new stars. I wondered how that affected his understanding of the familiar tale.

The deeper we dug, the more jewels the trunk delivered. An officer's card out of Maiduguri confirmed Dad's presence in deeper Africa as well as his continued journey toward India. Today, the rebel group, Boko Haram, dominates the news out of Maiduguri. Until discovering the trunk I hadn't realized I had family history there. A photo of a proud Dad kneeling beside a dead gazelle, along with others of fellow soldiers, of natives and of monkeys, gave me snippets of his downtime. He often posed without a shirt, maybe proud of his trim physique or simply trying to cool off.

In the bottom of the trunk lay the mother lode: a single sheet of yellowed paper with columns of printed information. As a pilot, Gary recognized it immediately as the five flight paths with coordinates from destinations in India to several in China. One column gave the departure stations and their elevations and tower coordinates, and then the same information for each town or radio beacon a pilot would have crossed over on the routes to China.

Misamari jumped out as the first station listed and was included on the "Able" and "Easy" courses, two of the routes over the Hump to Kunming, China. Mont Jennings had mentioned the Able route in his interview, but this official document was the first outside confirmation I had that Dad was deployed there. By saving this piece of paper that had guided him in his flying, Dad had personally delivered a gift that would now guide me on my trip. "I was here," he confirmed, bringing alive his experience. It was an important document for him to save and a godsend for our journey.

I would learn more about Dad from the contents of the trunk, but for this day, just knowing we were going to the correct place in India was enough. I didn't need to worry about what the transcript said about the name of the river in India. Our destination was secure.

THREE

Pioneer Life on the High Plains of Texas

It's Easter Sunday, April 14, 1935, a beautiful day with bright blue skies on the High Plains of Texas. Mom wakes me that morning with her usual, "Charlie, get up. You're going to church." My siblings and I were never given a choice on Sundays. Church it was. My family attends the only church in Cleo, Texas, an even smaller town than nearby Hart. The nine of us pile into the Dodge, the six bigger kids in back—three on the cushioned seats and three on the bench my father put in the middle. My brother Bruce gives the orders where everyone should sit. Our youngest sibling, Helen, rides up front with Mom and Dad.

A preacher from the seminary in Plainview conducts the service. Brother Ray gives a nice message about the rising of Jesus and its importance to our lives today. He gets a little carried away for my taste, but there are no other choices in Cleo.

The Houchens, a family with almost as many kids as ours, has invited us for lunch and Mom's bringing the lemon cake she made last night, a guaranteed favorite. At the Houchens house, we eat our fill of beef, potatoes, canned squash and beans, and corn bread. And, of course, Mom's cake. All washed down with sweet tea

About three in the afternoon, the distant clouds get very dark, darker than I've ever seen them. A black wall of clouds, filling the horizon, approaches, a terrifying sight. Thinking it a tornado cloud, Mr. Houchen insists we go to their storm shelter and wait for the storm to pass. As the winds arrive, I realize we're in an enormous tsunami of dust, an angry swirl of wind and dirt.

With his usual impatience, Dad decides we can't wait any longer, and our family braves the wind and dirt to get back into our car. Driving home is slow and tedious. Mom has to help drive from her passenger seat as my father rolls down his window to clear the windshield of dust with his hand. I wonder what will be left of our young wheat crop, just recently planted. At home, I can only wait with my family until the storm passes, the furniture and floors accumulating a heavy layer of dirt. I will have to use a shovel to help Mom push the dust out tomorrow. It will be a beautiful day. It always is after a storm like this.

Father with siblings in the family car. My father is seated on the running board, far left.

* * *

I WISH I could write that story from Dad's retelling of it. I wish I could write that my father loved to tell stories about his growing up, preferably funny ones. I would love just one that recounted when Dad tumbled a tractor into a ditch or bounced out of the bed of the family's pickup or even played hooky to get out of school and out of working on the farm. But my father never revealed details about his childhood, at least not to me or my brothers.

Without a father to quiz, stories of Dad's youth came from my grand-mother and aunts, especially Aunt Winnie Moore, my only surviving aunt when I began this journey. She provided the details of the Easter dust storm, the most famous storm of the Dust Bowl days. When I asked her about funny stories, she replied with one about my father losing control of the mules as he tried to plow a family field. Aunt Winnie laughed as she recalled the mules running off with Dad, who was desperately trying to round them up, maybe the first time he had been left alone to plow.

An early photograph of my father reveals a lanky, freckled child in torn overalls and bare feet staring frankly into the camera. No smile, but no scowl either. His eyes are engaged, possibly wondering how the camera worked. Other pictures captured him on the running board of the family car with a dapper hat; another, at work on a tractor or near a truck, always accompanied by his brothers. The photos hinted at stories never told.

Dad's youth spent on Texas farms mirrored that of many American boys. Farmers made up a fourth of the US work force in the 1920s. His pioneer family migrated to the Texas Panhandle from Hamlin, Texas where Dad had been born. I learned at my Uncle Bruce's funeral that they had been the first to plow the soil of Castro County as the High Plains began to attract farmers with its rich, flat lands. Wheat and cotton dominated the crops.

My grandfather was also the first in the area to get a tractor, and all the farmers around came by to see it in action. Granddad worked three sections of land, two rented and one owned. That's over eighteen hundred acres of land and he must have realized that he had to take a chance on the new tractor if so much land was going to be made productive.

Aunt Helen was guardian of the family photos during her lifetime and was generous in sharing them with her nieces and nephews before her death. It was surprising how many black-and-white photos she had accumulated from the farm years. Back then, roving photographers would capture posed moments of life on the family farm.

A favorite photograph of mine from Helen's collection was a take on Grant Wood's American Gothic, with father and mother behind their children, all lined up in front of a wooden farmhouse. In the Walker version, my youngest aunt's presence is visible under my grandmother's dress as my grandmother is noticeably pregnant with her last child. A giant of a man stands to the side, later identified as the family's only "hired hand." He dwarfs my grandfather. To the left are the three boys: Preston, Bruce and Charles (my father), all of whom used their middle name with an initial for the first name, a common practice at the time—J. Preston, R. Bruce and R. Charles. Next are the girls—Lucy and the twins, Lennie and Winnie—named after my grandmother's sisters.

Also in the photo is my paternal great-grandmother, looking dour and ancient, but possibly only in her sixties. No one looks happy, especially my grandmother, who often complained of her hard work raising seven children in an isolated home with no help from either my grandfather or her mother-in-law. Among the many challenges were Dust Bowl storms like the one I described, which coated a house inside and out with a fine layer of topsoil.

A rare source of family history came via my cousin, who filmed my grandmother when she was in her nineties talking about early farm life. They always had a large garden, filled with vegetables to be canned for the winter. As each year's flock of chickens matured, my grandmother fried chicken, a summer treat. Pigs and cows were slaughtered to make sausage for the winter. The family never lacked for food. In the video, my grandmother doesn't have much nice to say about her husband, making me wonder about the dynamics of my grandparents' relationship and how it affected the children. Dad's father died when I was three and was not a part of my growing up. Just as he never talked about his youth, Dad never talked about his father.

The family moved from farm to farm, eventually also getting a town home in Plainview to be closer to schools. In a show of confidence in their boys, my grandparents allowed Dad and his brothers to live alone in the Plainview house to go to high school; the boys had to walk two miles to

My father's family on the farm. He's the third boy from the left.

school to avoid paying ten cents for the bus. They returned to working on the farm during summers.

Aunt Winnie gave me insight into her brothers' characters as children: The oldest, Preston, was the sweetest; Bruce, next in line, was bossy; and my father had the "best personality." I loved hearing that, wishing I could have identified that trait of my dad's in later life. As the youngest boy, Dad liked to tease his younger sisters. From an early age, he also loved airplanes and would ride his bike to a hobby shop to buy model planes. My brothers later rode to that same shop, probably encouraged by Dad. After the war, Dad could have easily identified the models my brothers put together.

All seven Walker children graduated high school, indicating a strong commitment by my grandparents to learning. Hoping Plainview High School kept old school records, I wrote for a copy of Dad's transcript. Its receipt in the mail was an unexpected primary source. As usual, I felt like an intruder. Would I want my children to see my report card? I had never thought of researching family history as having an ethical component, yet I often felt like an eavesdropper as I discovered information about Dad without his knowledge. My mother had always wondered how she and Dad could have produced such smart children since neither of them was a strong student. She was right to be curious. According to his records, Dad was a lackluster student, especially in his earlier years, barely scraping through English and Algebra and failing a semester of Spanish. But the grades improved in his last two years, with agriculture being his strongest subject.

One trait stood out from his years in school: After his freshman year, he never missed a class. He had many opportunities to skip. Snowy days or dust storms. Work needed on the farm. Lack of interest. Childhood illness. But Aunt Winnie confirmed that there simply wasn't a choice. Their parents expected them all to go to school, and that was that.

I realized I didn't ever remember Dad being sick or staying home from work. He could have worked through his illness without me knowing, but it seemed more likely he was just a healthy guy. His four sisters and one brother lived into their nineties. My paternal grandmother celebrated her hundredth birthday two months before her death. Hard work and country living may have imbued the family with a strong immunity to viruses.

My other guess on Dad's near-perfect attendance in high school was his interest in learning. His grades didn't reflect it, but he may not have had much to time to study. History was his second-best subject, helping explain his fascination with museums. When visiting historical museums on our family trips, we always had to wait for Dad to finish, a trait my older brother and I inherited and one that might have unconsciously contributed to my later decision to major in history in college.

Dad appeared to be a curious guy and he chose to continue educating himself after high school. It was a period of increased secondary education in the US, yet relatively few high school graduates advanced to college. Dad did. The nearby Texas Technological College in Lubbock had opened in 1925 with agriculture as one of its four focuses and, apparently, a low bar for admission. My father never bragged about his AG degree from Texas Tech, but he should have been proud. At the time only six percent of white male Americans graduated from college. He was the only son in the family to get a degree but was eventually joined by two of his sisters.

While at Texas Tech, Dad got lucky. President Roosevelt was aware that only some nine thousand private pilot licenses were being issued each year in the U.S. and that the country was going to need many more pilots for the impending war. He established the Civilian Pilot Training Program to train college students to fly, a program that would double the numbers of new pilots. Texas Tech was one of many universities selected to offer the training, and the Civil Aeronautics Authority paid the $290 tuition for the flight course. The timing of this program, 1939-40, coincided with my father's final year at Texas Tech, and when I read about it, I imagined Dad jumping at this opportunity to follow his love of airplanes and learn to fly, especially as he wouldn't have had that kind of money to pay for the course himself, at least according to Aunt Winnie. My hunch was right: Dad's college transcript revealed credit for the Civilian Pilot Training program.

Getting a pilot's license in 1940 put Dad into an elite group, an early achievement for a small-town farm boy. Whether or not he knew that war was coming, his embrace of flight school set the stage for Dad's World War II experience. By the time he entered the service at age twenty-six, my father had been flying for years.

My father on far right with his older brothers, Bruce and Preston, on the farm.

FOUR

Dear Ace Charlie: Letters to a Favorite Instructor

"I hope we all make good so that someday you'll be proud of us."
>—Letter dated May 11, 1942 from Richard Vickrey, who wrote my father three times and would run into him in Africa two years later

"I appreciate your invitation to go on a deer hunt."
>—Letter dated November 24, 1942 from Quentin Goss

"I hope you get the subscription to Esquire."
>—Letter dated December 19, 1942 from Daniel Steen

* * *

AFTER DISCOVERING THE letters from Dad's flying students in his World War II trunk, I carefully carried them home to read, knowing they were irreplaceable, hoping each would evoke Dad's presence…his past…a part of him. The letters were an unexpected connection to my father, hidden away all these years, just waiting for the right person to find them, probably wondering if they would ever be discovered by a family who had never explored its father's past. They must have felt like giving up, deciding that their treasure of heartfelt sentiments was not important, was dated, passé. I was about to liberate their contents, to place them front and center on the journey to find Dad.

In preparing to read the letters, I chose my time carefully, not wanting to be interrupted. I felt I had a date with Dad, and I wanted him to myself. Sitting cross-legged on my office couch, I put the forty letters in chronological order, carefully examining each envelope and letter, noting the return addresses of thirteen different bases, either the "free" written in the stamp corner of many or an Army Defense three-cent stamp, and Dad's name and succinct address, sometimes just Uvalde, Texas. The envelopes were faded and yellowed but in good condition, probably unopened since the war's end. Some had a funny reminder printed on them: "Pull rip cord right and down." Most were written on personalized stationery with the solder's name and posting printed at the top. As they progressed in their training, stationery was provided at each new posting, an indication of the importance of this way of communication during the war. The soldiers' legible handwriting, proper grammar and punctuation reflected the emphasis on those skills in elementary schools, skills that stood out for me, given the lack of importance given them in modern-day texts and dictated messages.

In the early years of the war, Dad worked for Hanger 6, a company that provided aviation instructors for the US Army. At the time the aviation industry was growing but there were only thirty-one thousand men and women—mostly men—licensed to fly in the United States. Thousands more were needed, and quickly. Dad had been flying since he was in college and, evidently, three years of flying experience was enough to teach others. He worked out of Uvalde, one of thirty-six sites in Texas where pilots were being trained for the war effort. Classes of six new recruits were assigned to each instructor. Dad was not yet in the Army and that seemed to give him more flexibility in befriending his students than the career Army instructors who used fear tactics to train student pilots and who often pulled rank.

Dad's class was for beginners, the primary stage. They soloed first in a PT-19A, a simple flying machine made partially out of plywood—a detail that may have concerned my father, but one that allowed for cheaper production. It couldn't fly faster than 132 mph, but mastering it was considered the first stop toward becoming a combat pilot. After passing Dad's requirements, the students progressed to larger, faster and more complicated planes with a bewildering array of new letters and numbers attached to

Envelope from stack of students' letters sent to my father in Uvalde, Texas.

their names, such as the BT-13A, the A-6 or the more advanced fighter plane, P-36. They would also have to learn cross-country techniques, night flying, and how to pull out of stalls caused when the nose of an airplane pitched too high and the plane lost its lift. Instrument flying was introduced in later classes. But it all began in Dad's class.

I started to read the letters—slowly, deliberately, with anticipation and with hope for personal insights into my father. I felt his eyes over my shoulder, scanning the letters, remembering each student, smiling at their stories, taking him back to the early war days. I wanted him there with me to identify each one and what the student meant to him. I wanted him to add stories to theirs. These were men who knew him, admired him and were influenced by him. They were young and, at twenty-six Dad was just enough older to be a mentor. I couldn't have my father's side of the correspondence, yet these students, now all dead, were about to speak from the past and teach me about my father as a young man.

My father (*in the back, center*) with four of his pilot students. On the far left in the back row is Gene Rutledge, whom Dad would later introduce to his sister, and they would marry.

The first of the forty letters was dated May 12, 1942 and the last, December 20, 1943, the communication continuing well after Dad finished instructing. From these letters, I learned that he was a responsive correspondent. Several noted how quickly Dad replied to their letters. Some apologized for being so late in responding. Much of their postal conversation centered on planes; "ships," as many called them. Technical references to types of planes and their flying idiosyncrasies were beyond my knowledge but clearly not my father's. I began to recognize individual names as their correspondence stretched over several months and postings. One soldier wrote him six times, another five times; many, two and three times. Receipt of a student's graduation notice, meaning he had earned his wings, was common.

A playful side of my father ran through many of the letters. An inside joke in one of Dad's groups was the naming of each other as "ace" and referring to the group as the Ace Club, possibly a holdover from World War I's use of the term "ace pilot." When they wrote Dad, they would refer to Ace Warren drawing a BT-13 to fly, Ace Mullen getting the BT-14 and Ace Goss flying the AT-6. They even addressed Dad as Ace Walker. Another set of students referred to themselves as Dad's "dodos," kidding him about their progress, or maybe lack of progress. More than one wanted him to join up and become a part of their unit. One even sent him a subscription to Esquire. These guys liked Dad a lot.

The letters contained gossip about other students, complaints about instructors, pride in conquering each new step, fear of missing airports or making poor landings, and much admiration for Dad as a teacher and person. From them, I learned that Dad had patience, was complimentary, liked to kid around and that his office was always open. Many wished they could get back to Uvalde to walk into that office for a good chat. He took the fear out of their first assignment, even as later army instructors gave it back. Del Geary confirmed this in his January 13, 1943 letter, in which he wrote, "I wouldn't recommend you change anything [about teaching] because I can still look back and say I had a good instructor once." The students clearly preferred Dad's method, as would I.

Quentin Goss seemed to have a special relationship with Dad, with my father acting as a counselor. His six letters were filled with much detail about the planes he was flying, but also with personal concerns. He couldn't decide which direction to go in with his training—fighter pilot, pursuit, light or heavy bombardment, transport, or armed reconnaissance. I hadn't realized there were so many choices. Goss asked for Dad's input, and a later letter revealed that Dad had suggested taking on the heavy airplanes. I discovered from a Google search that Goss would go on to graduate from West Point and be one of the first fighter pilots to cross the English Channel on D-Day; after the war, he worked in Air Force Systems Command. But in 1943 Goss showed a vulnerable side as he sought my father's guidance. His letters allowed me to experience Dad's influence on Goss's success. I wondered if his correspondence with Dad continued after the war.

Despite the passage of time, I felt I was prying into the open-hearted, honest disclosures being made to Dad by young and scared new pilots. They admitted their fears, including worries about washing out, concerns of missing towns on night excursions, nervousness about slow adjustments to the next level of planes, and problems with taming vertigo or anxiety. I was saddened to read of the death of one of his students even before he got to the war zones. In a letter dated June 23, 1942, Harold Filgo wrote, "I guess Vickrey told you about Mr. Cray's crack-up. He spun in with full throttle, according to reports. They certainly had some pretty flowers at the funeral. The prettiest thing was a pair of wings about 5 feet long made of white roses." That letter must have shaken Dad up.

Their letters were unfiltered and filled with fresh observations about the war and about flying, planes, instructors and other students. Two wrote just before they shipped out, their uneasiness reflected in the short letters. Joe R. Foote wrote on November 19, 1942: "At last I am going into the war zone. Don't know for sure what we'll have to fly... Heard the news yesterday and today getting things ready... Wish me luck." Seventy-five years later, I wanted to wish him luck myself.

Even without access to Dad's own letters, the students' correspondence gave a picture of my young father: already an accomplished pilot, supervising fresh recruits being introduced to the world of flying. By writing them often, his concern was obvious. He could have cut them loose after his classes, but he didn't. They replied to his letters, asking about other students and what planes they hoped to fly. The letters revealed an outgoing and playful personality that I had seldom seen.

My father also could have sealed them off from his personal life, but he didn't. I chuckled in recognition at Dad's outreach: an invitation for a student to join him for a deer hunt and his attempt to hook up another with a girl he knew. Quentin Goss wrote that he hadn't had time to look up the girl Dad had suggested, but that he intended to. My father later introduced one of his students, Gene Rutledge, to my Aunt Lennie, and they married. This has been a lifelong tendency of mine—to bring people together, to make them feel welcome, to host newcomers for dinner. My husband and I even had a "singles" party when we lived in Houston to introduce all the single young people we knew at the time. We brought together my best friend with his best friend and they married. I loved learning that Dad worked his relationships in the same way—welcoming and inclusive, clever/devious in his introductions, always networking.

When I was growing up, it was my mother who seemed to have the most friends, the ready smile, the connections to school classmates, the most sociability. I'm a lot like her. But maybe I just assume this to be so because I got to know her as an adult. From the letters, I learned that Dad also had many of these characteristics. His openness to new relationships mirrors mine: meeting new people, getting their stories, staying in touch. And his approach to teaching reflects my favorite style of leadership: positive reinforcement. These discoveries brought us closer, even if it was now only on my side.

Regretfully, I put down the last letter, this one dated December 20, 1943 from Quentin Goss. By that time, Dad was in the army too, and the letter was addressed to Lt. R.C. Walker at his Love Field, Dallas address. Quentin hoped that "Santa leaves you the ship you want. I asked for a P-57." They were still talking planes. He signed off, "Be seeing you."

I sat quietly with the letters surrounding me, feeling as if I had just sent these men off to war. And I was despondent that the direct connection with Dad had ended. For a few brief hours I'd had my father with me again, a crack in the years of silence, opened by those who knew him in a different way. Each letter was an unintentional gift from a new soldier who was just writing a favorite teacher, not realizing it would later introduce a daughter to her father's past. Each letter had been a spotlight on Dad, a genuine interaction with him, helping to paint a picture of a caring and capable instructor and friend. I would never know that part of Dad personally, but it was an unexpected joy to experience it through his students.

This must have been a positive experience for Dad too, as he kept the letters in his trunk after the war. I wondered—and I'm sure Dad did too—about the later war history of those who wrote him. After Dad left Uvalde, his address changed many times, from Love Field to St. Louis and overseas to Ghana, Nigeria and India. No other letters from his pilots were in the trunk, a reflection of his mobility and theirs.

I now like to think that Dad's efforts and encouragement contributed in a personal way to the success of many Army pilots, even after they left Uvalde. His was a small cog in the World War II wheel, mirrored by many other instructors. But if the letters reflect his ability as a teacher, he was successful.

"All the things you taught me about flying a PT was the best background in the world for flying a BT-13. If I don't make it, it won't be because of my primary training but because I didn't keep my head out."

—The only letter from Joe B. Warren, August 24, 1942

FIVE

An Absent Father

• *It is June 1959 and my brothers are playing baseball in Little League. Mom keeps a complicated calendar with all the games listed. There are no sports for girls, and I can only tag along to the games. With some of the games extending into the evening, Mom often packs sandwiches for dinner at the ballpark. One evening as the sun is setting, I see my father walk up to the stands and climb in beside Mom. This rarely happens. My brothers must often recount the games to Dad back home when he finally comes in. I know Mack and Gary will be excited that he's here.*

• *It is early one summer morning in 1960. Mom wants to get on the road. She's driving us five children to Denver in her Plymouth station wagon—one child in front, two in the middle and two in the third seat facing backwards. No room is made for Dad. He's staying home. With the crops nearing maturity, his presence is required on the farm. Dad has promised to fly up in his plane in a few days to enjoy Denver with us. But he will return early, leaving Mom to get us back home. This is not an unusual arrangement and I think it normal for my mother to drive the five hundred miles alone. Mom doesn't complain. She's used to it and knows that if she wants to travel in the summer, she must be willing to do it alone at times. We get off by eight and drive to Colorado Springs for the first night.*

• *It is February 1964. Mom and Dad are hosting their monthly bridge club. But it's only my mother and me setting up the tables and putting out the food and drinks. As the time of the party approaches, Mom makes a quick call to the shed, trying to locate my father. He finally arrives and walks quickly back to shower. I hear him dressing as the first guests ring the doorbell. Mom welcomes them and makes small talk until Dad can slip into the party, taking over the duties of serving drinks.*

* * *

I OFTEN WONDER if my mother knew what it would mean to marry a farmer. Was she aware of the long hours required nine months of the year to plant, grow and harvest a crop? Did she support his growing businesses even if it meant regular absences from the family? How patient was she when he arrived late to an event, or not at all? In reflecting on their lives together, I was surprised to discover a depth of experiences despite Dad's scarce presence.

Both my parents grew up in or near Plainview—Dad on a farm and Mom "in town." My mother was three years younger, the same age as Dad's twin sisters, and their families lived only blocks apart. In a small town, this proximity in age and distance meant that each knew who the other was, even before the war.

During World War II, Mom worked in Dallas and volunteered with the Red Cross to do her part for the war effort. Love Field was a busy army base then and many soldiers passed through. Mom loved to dance, and she joined other young women attending dances sponsored by the USO to cheer up the soldiers, even if that meant taking a long bus ride home across town at night after the dance. It was no surprise that she also dated some of these young men, including Dad, who was stationed at Love Field for a few months. But then my father disappeared for fourteen months to serve abroad, a harbinger of his later absences.

After the war my parents reconnected. I don't know the story—maybe through Dad's sisters; maybe because Mom was available and Dad was interested; maybe because Mom lived in Dallas when Dad was stationed there again before being discharged and returning to Plainview.

Dad had to pursue Mom, as he was not her only suitor. I imagine Mom was attracted to Dad's exciting war experiences (Mom was always tearfully patriotic), his intellect as evidenced by his college degree, a high energy that matched hers, and his dreams. Even then, Dad was surely thinking ahead to his next steps—buying a farm, trying new crops, opening a chemical and crop-dusting business and exploring other opportunities in Plainview. Both Mom's parents died young and I think Mom needed Dad's confidence the most, to be assured that she was marrying a reliable man and that returning to Plainview would be okay. She admitted that Dad had to press her to marry him with a threat of cutting off the relationship. She "finally realized how special he was," as she told me once, and they married on June 7, 1948.

At least that was the story I knew until I found the "love letter" in Dad's World War II trunk, addressed to him while he was stationed in India and flying the Hump. Margie from Wichita wrote him a rather subdued letter in March 1945, without even a "Dear Charlie" salutation. Composed as a poem, the letter recalled a fond Easter weekend the year before when they had worshiped together, eaten, walked, gone to a movie and kissed. It closed with "Love, Margie." As I read and reread the poem, I felt like a voyeur, peering in on a Sunday outing between Dad and a woman he obviously liked. It was hard to imagine Dad with a woman other than my mother. My brothers were also surprised to learn of another love interest. Even though it wasn't a passionate letter, suggesting that perhaps it wasn't a passionate encounter, I'm confident Dad would have been happy to recall that Easter as he climbed into the cockpit for another flight across the Himalayas, a memory to sustain him during the months abroad.

Also in the trunk was a large eight-by-ten photo of an unknown woman, possibly Margie. She had come to Texas to visit after the war, and my father's family thought this "other woman" was his love interest. But Dad must have been keeping his options open, as his family didn't even know he was dating my mother at that same time. Aunt Winnie revealed that Dad managed to startle his family with his decision to marry Mom. I laughed at this, remembering how my brothers and even my son have kept important parts of their lives to themselves until they absolutely had to reveal them, including where they were going to college or when they intended to marry.

After discovering the second woman, I had so many unanswerable questions. Was she why Dad wanted a decision from Mom? Would he have married Margie if Mom had refused to decide or had turned him down? Had Mom known about her? Dad was twenty-eight when he exited the service and wanted to settle down. It seemed that everyone else had returned home and married, including his brother Bruce and two of his sisters. The war had delayed that part of his life. Now he was back in Plainview and needed a wife and, apparently, he was going to get one, even if it meant playing one girlfriend against another. In other photos that we've since discovered, Dad must have dated several women during the war, photos that showed his arm around a waist or holding a hand. This was a side of Dad I never knew, and I had to admire his determination.

The wedding was small, with only a few family members and friends from Plainview and Dallas attending. Looking at the wedding photos, I noted that Dad wasn't wearing his military uniform or a suit, preferring a tuxedo, an early indication of his later sharp dressing. Dad always looked good, keeping his closet neat and tidy, with suits separate from his work clothes, shirts ironed, pant creases crisply folded. As remembered by Aunt Winnie, he had a special fondness for jackets, an observation that applies to my closet as well, an unexpected connection to Dad. And careful examination of his facial features in the photos confirms our resemblance, with thin lips, sharp nose, freckled skin; I'm also thin and short, as he was. His close haircut continued for the rest of his life.

Dad's brother-in-law Hall Nall (his real name) was his best man. Another photo shows the two of them standing outside the church, smiling and with cigarettes in hand, waiting for the service to begin. As my cousin Lance Nall describes it, "Two young cocky guys in their prime, knowing they had paid their dues in the war and ready to enjoy life." In the wedding party photo, both my parents smile broadly, clearly happy with the decision to marry. It must have felt like a new beginning, a welcome moment after years of Depression and war. Even as I observed the bliss of the moment in the photo, I felt strangely anxious for them both, knowing what lay ahead. Nothing could change the outcome, yet I felt protective, wishing I could warn them somehow.

As with most postwar families, my parents' life in Plainview filled quickly with babies arriving every year or two, along with Dad's emerging business interests, Mom's tendency to volunteer for children's and church activities and a large extended family on both sides, leaving them little

My parents' wedding photo June 7, 1947.

time to themselves. They were modestly affectionate with each other. My cousin Carolyn remembers that Dad kissed Mom every time he came home, something her parents never did and an act I took for granted. I didn't recognize it as anything special until Carolyn's observation. In the summer, I remember Dad dropping by the house for lunch most days, eating quickly and taking a short nap to make up for the early morning awakenings. I realize now that in the winter, when we children were in school, this midday encounter with Mom would have been a time for easy and open conversation and, possibly, intimacy.

I loved it when my parents entertained with dinner parties or bridge games—the buzz of the conversation, elevated voices after a drink or two, laughter at a story well told. Their bridge group met as often for partying as for card-playing. The gathering after Mom and Dad returned from Mexico with a recipe for a new drink called the margarita was particularly loud and boisterous. I could hear the fun as I lay in bed, unable to sleep until the guests departed.

One fall evening in 1962, Mom walked back to the family room, a mischievous smile on her face, and asked Mack and me to demonstrate the twist to the party in the living room. The newest dance move was all the craze. While I knew my mother loved to dance, the twist was very different from the jitterbug, swing and the waltz that my parents' generation grew up with. Couples no longer joined hands. Each dancer was on his or her own. Neither Mack nor I was excited to dance in front of Mom and Dad's friends but agreed to after Mom's enthusiastic encouragement.

We brought our record player into the living room and put on Chubby Checker, whose song had started the craze. The twist was not a complicated dance, requiring only a swivel of the hips and moves backwards and forwards and occasionally down and up, and I was surprised that these adults couldn't figure that out. Mack and I danced one song together to get them started, feeling a bit awkward with so many eyes on us. Soon every couple was up, a few catching on immediately but most having trouble making their hips move properly, especially the men. All were laughing, including Dad. I couldn't get over distinguished Dr. Heye, proper Mrs. Williams and even my Sunday School teacher being so relaxed and even silly. The party revealed the lively relationship my parents had when Dad was present and both were relaxed, and it felt like an introduction to how fun adult life just might be.

There were rare arguments, raised voices behind closed doors in the bedroom. Nothing violent. Nothing thrown. My bedroom was the closest to theirs and I was the only one to hear the change of tenor in their voices. I can't be certain why they argued—possibly over his new plane, his many absences, his failure to share feelings, her over-involvement as a volunteer or the general chaos of the home. I knew it was more serious when a cuss word rang out above the muffled voices.

Yet neither of my parents seemed to carry the tension of an argument into the next day, and they never shared any of their marriage frustrations with me or my brothers. I didn't appreciate the fact that they kept their differences private until I talked to friends or read books by authors whose parents often fought in front of them as kids. For me, it was a previously unacknowledged gift of parent-modeling that carried over to my relationship with my husband and our children.

Early on, Dad's flying caused friction, if only because he continued to crop dust, a hazardous method of controlling weeds and insects. He had started his crop dusting business soon after returning from the war. The process then was rudimentary when compared to today's computerized flying: Two men, often my maternal uncles, would each hold a flag at a corner of the field as Dad lined up the plane and the chemicals to be sure they were dropped on the correct farm…and hopefully not on my uncles. Avoiding buildings and electric lines was the biggest challenge. Mom didn't want him taking such big chances with so many children at home.

My cousin Ronnie Walker told the story of his father, my Uncle Bruce, being approached by a deputy sheriff one day on his farm. The officer told Bruce that there had been a crop-dusting accident, that a man had been killed and that they thought it was my dad. They needed Bruce to identify the body. When Bruce and the deputy sheriff arrived at the accident site, they saw that the pilot had been burned beyond recognition; however, he was wearing a ring. Bruce knew that it wasn't Dad's wedding ring, and Dad was located soon after. Until Ronnie shared it, I had never heard this story, and I'm sure it was one that greatly frightened my mother. Possibly because of incidents like this one, Dad finally stopped crop-dusting.

Judging by the growing numbers of businesses that Dad was accumulating, he must have been a savvy entrepreneur, putting together all the many moving parts for an integrated business model: land for farming, a chemical company to provide needed chemicals for spraying weeds and insects, a shed to process the harvested produce and an ice company to provide ice to cool the sacked produce in the railcars. As Ronnie pointed out, an "empire" like that "didn't come easily." It would have required much time away from the family, my father's major failing according to today's parenting standards.

I was aware of my father's business expansions, but I had never put them together as a plan that my father must have always had.

My mother's independent nature served her well, being married to an entrepreneur who was often absent. She immersed herself in her children's activities, being the occasional room mother and constant chauffeur, and prepared three meals a day, along with picnics for little league games. All of this required an organizational ability few mothers of the time likely had, but mine did. And she seemed to enjoy it, creating the family life she missed growing up.

I don't remember any negative comments from Mom about Dad's regular disappearances. He wouldn't even stay long at his own family's gatherings, dropping in to say hello, then moving on. I considered it normal for Dad to miss or be only partially present during my school assemblies and band concerts, and for those basketball games where I performed as a twirler. I would never expect him to pick me up at school or help with homework. Mom managed to take up the slack and did it all. This wasn't unusual for the times. Many fathers took a hands-off approach to childrearing, even when they were more physically present than Dad was.

Mom was the first line when it came to discipline, and counting slowly to ten usually did the trick. For particularly serious infractions, Dad was called in for spankings after he got home from work. Waiting for his usual late arrival was worse than the punishment, as his paddles were more for show than hurt. Still, I hated that experience so much that it influenced my decision to never paddle my children.

We traveled in the US every summer, Mom at the wheel of her trusty old Plymouth station wagon—at first with a mattress in the far back and the luggage on top and later with a third seat. Dad occasionally participated fully in our travels, but more often chose to fly up to our destination for a few days and then return quickly. He claimed the farm needed his attention during those summer trips. Maybe. Or maybe it was the constant fights over who crossed the line into another sibling's territory in the car. Maybe it was one too many "are we there yet?" questions. Maybe he preferred a good night's sleep, as opposed to sharing one hotel room with five children and a wife, all somehow spread out over two double beds and the floor. Or maybe he just needed time to himself. Mom could put up with all that. Travel was that important to her.

Photo of family on a road trip when my father has joined us. *Left to right*:
Me, Jeff, Gary, Morey, Mack, my mother, and my father.

We explored Washington, DC, Los Angeles, Denver and Seattle, we
hiked in National Parks and swam in lakes and oceans. I tried new sports
like snow skiing, surfing and horseback riding, experiences unavailable in
the Texas Panhandle. My parents weren't afraid of the world, so neither
was I. Many friends' families always vacationed in the same place every
year. Some never traveled. Our destination changed each year. Without
benefit of the internet and apps, I learned to read a map. Today, all my
brothers and I have a good sense of direction, maybe inherited and maybe
learned. Watching my parents get lost in an unfamiliar city provided a
model of problem-solving—working together to find their way, reorienting
themselves, using observations to get right again. My favorite story of

truly getting lost was in the spokes of the Washington, DC street grid. We were in the car, trying to get to the National Cathedral but Dad kept getting pulled back to the city center instead of out to where the church was located. Mom saw a nun in a cab and yelled out to follow her. Dad did, and the cab took us directly to the cathedral. Now, whenever any of us is lost, we encourage the others to look for the nun!

Once Dad bought his six-seater Bonanza plane, he not only used it for business, he also started flying the family for weekends in Dallas or to more distant destinations. He became more present in our lives with these trips, more willing to join us, less likely to stay home. His control of the schedule probably contributed to his willingness to come along.

Dad must have loved Mom a lot because he joined the Episcopal church for her, a move not appreciated by his family. The Episcopal church was just a little too close to Catholic, a deeply suspicious religion for the majority Baptist and Church of Christ population of Plainview. Surprisingly, Dad always attended Sunday services with us, but he often missed extras like Ash Wednesday and Good Friday. These were unfamiliar services to him, and he could use work as a reason to skip them, his usual excuse for being absent. Neither of my parents talked to us about God or about being saved by Jesus, despite both having been raised Southern Baptist. Guilting wasn't their style. I guess they hoped Sunday School and church services would do the trick. In retrospect, I feel as though they left us free to find our own way in spiritual matters.

Scattered around Mom's kitchen were funny signs she picked up on her travels, like "Try Our World-Famous Peanut Butter and Jelly Sandwiches" or "God, Put Your Arm Around My Shoulders and Your Hand Over My Mouth." I knew Mom's sense of humor but not Dad's. He always seemed to have a slight smile on his face, but I can't think of a time when he laughed out loud. Another plaque on the wall introduced us to Reinhold Niebuhr's "Serenity Prayer": "God give me the serenity to accept the things I cannot change, the courage to change the things I can, and the wisdom to know the difference." After my father's death, Mom often looked up at this prayer on the wall, briefly reflecting on it, hoping it would help ease my Dad's now-permanent absence.

SIX

War Letter from Africa

"Say you low down skunk. I wrote you after I got over here but maybe the darn letter never got to you. Yours went all over the world before it got here."

—Letter dated December 6, 1944 from Dad
to Gene Rutledge, postmarked Maiduguri, Nigeria

* * *

DESPITE MANY REFERENCES to Dad's letters among the student letters in the World War II trunk, I had none from him. Clearly, he was a dedicated correspondent, replying quickly to letters he received. Many students apologized for taking so long to write, especially as Dad had so efficiently responded to their letters.

One of Dad's students was my uncle Gene Rutledge. He wouldn't be part of the family for several more years, when he married my Aunt Lennie. Because they lived several hundred miles away in southeast Texas, I seldom saw him. But I knew he always loved my father because of their war connection. The last time I saw him was at a rare visit he made to Plainview, to attend Dad's funeral. As part of my research, I reached out to his family's historian—his son David—for memories of Dad and asked whether he had heard any war stories from his father about mine.

David had two surprises for me. The first was personal: "Uncle Charlie was my favorite uncle. He was everyone's favorite uncle." I had heard the same declaration from my cousin Barbara. Once again, it took me by surprise. How could I have missed that admiration over the years? It made me feel good and yet embarrassed at my lack of observation. Pride mixed with frustration.

Unfortunately, David had no stories about Dad, other than Gene had loved him. But he did have a letter from my father to his father, the second surprise, and he offered to send a copy. After reading so many letters to Dad, I had lost hope of ever finding one from him. I jumped up at the discovery, running downstairs to deliver the news to my husband. It would have been nice to hold the original, but David didn't want to let it go because it was the only correspondence he had from Uncle Charlie. In return, I offered to share with him the announcement of his father graduating from flight school that I found among the letters in Dad's trunk. It was a rare and powerful exchange of our fathers' history, passing in the mail.

I lingered over the envelope from David, knowing what lay inside. At last, I was making direct contact with Dad. I felt excited, yet anxious. Would it be a disappointment? Would it live up to my expectations? What would I learn about him? How honest would he be? Not surprisingly, these were the same questions I had asked about the letters to Dad from his students. Just as Native Americans often give thanks to plants before using them for sustenance, I thanked Dad for writing the letter and pulled it out of the envelope.

The brief letter was the most intimate of all the clues left by Dad, a unique first source from the source, his voice speaking from the past. The handwriting tilted to the right, smallish with a sense of urgency, and filled two pages of personalized army stationery in straight lines. Since grammar was emphasized in my schooling, I always take note of a writer's grammar and I couldn't help doing the same thing with my father's. His sentences were mostly complete, paragraphs appropriate and verbs grammatically correct, with a smattering of exclamation marks and a few missing commas.

His tone was upbeat, greeting Gene with, "Say you low down skunk," and gently chastising him for not writing: "Maybe the darn letter never got to you." He ended the letter with a breezy, "So long, Charlie." In between was a treasure trove of information that, for the first time, directly pinpointed Dad in a specific place on a specific date: He confirmed his presence "in the center of Africa" on December 6, 1944, and the APO and Base Unit noted on the return address was in Maiduguri, Nigeria, the same APO and Base Unit referenced in the Christmas program and officers' card we found in his trunk. Before this letter, I could only guess when or where he was, based on outside sources.

Also in the letter, Dad asked Gene whether he planned to return home or keep flying combat missions. Thanks to the letters in the trunk, I recognized the reference to my father's long-time penpal student, Richard Vickrey, who had just passed through Africa on his way to China. Dad was "sure glad to see him." Vickrey had written my father often after graduating, complimenting Dad as being a "mighty nice man for an instructor."

Dad seemed proud of having been checked out to fly the C-46 and C-47, both of which he would later pilot over the Hump. In self-deprecating language, he claimed that it was a "routine job even an Army pilot can do," adding "ha ha!"—an Army inside joke, I guess.

I lingered uncomfortably over one paragraph, where he talked about the women in Africa, "where a white girl is something you dream about and the black well—!! I am glad to see you are in France and wish I could trade places with you at least until I can get satisfied again." Here was Dad as a young man looking for action, action that he had had before. Was Dad degrading black women with two exclamation marks? In a box of war photos, I found a black and white picture of an African naked woman staring directly into the camera. Other photos reflected bare chested African women with a wrap-around skirt. I didn't want to think him a racist or possibly frequenting a brothel. Maybe he just picked up a girl here and there. It certainly happened during the war years. I could justify it as Dad being a product of his time, especially since I don't remember Dad using racial slurs or demeaning women. Did he think differently of blacks? While there were few blacks in Plainview at the time, he did grow up in Texas, a state aligned more with the South than the North. Maybe it was wartime chatter. Trying to make light of a foreign post. Guys being guys. Dad being real. I will never know for certain.

Even so, so much of the puzzle came together with that single letter. Dad's presence in Africa, the planes he was trained to fly, his confirmation that he hoped to be back in the States in six more months: His path across the world map was filling in. The letter also touched on parts of Dad's personality. Compassionate—staying in touch with his students, such as Vickery ("sure glad to see him"), and inquiring about Gene's plans for more

One of my father's photos from his time in Africa, 1944.

combat work. Competent—getting checked out on the C-46 and C-47 was harder than Dad let on and would give many pilots challenges flying over the Hump; he played it down. Fun-loving—missing the kidding around previously allowed to instructors during his teaching days.

This didn't appear to be a man suffering war's tragedies, especially compared to the conflict raging in the European theater at that time. I know he found ways to enjoy himself. He appeared to be a regular at the officer's club in Maiduguri. He took advantage of hunting opportunities. The Thanksgiving and Christmas menus in the trunk would have cheered him up, especially the wine and beer. Maybe Dad was lonely and masking it with light banter. Maybe he was anxious about the next assignment to the Hump. I won't ever really know. But for that moment in time, Dad seemed to be okay and the letter reflected his contentment.

SEVEN

Being Different

"Charlie was different," Aunt Winnie replies to my request to describe my father. "He was just different."

"How different?" I ask.

"He joined the Boy Scouts. No one else was in Boy Scouts. That was a new organization and Charlie wanted to try it."

"Was there anything else?"

"He loved flying from an early age. He would ride his bicycle to the hobby shop and get plane models to make. He always wanted to try anything new. And he got a college degree. That was unusual. Charlie was just different."

* * *

DAD AND I shared more characteristics than I knew when I started this journey. Three times in a long-distance conversation that I initiated, Aunt Winnie described Dad as different. She would repeat it in later visits we had. Other adjectives flowed from this idea: curious…an inquiring and discerning mind…open to new ideas and inventions. I can peg other memories that match this description. He wore blue suits, not the standard black or brown. He drove the only white Plymouth Fury in town, not a typical farmer's pickup. He had one of the first pecan orchards in the area. The list started piling up.

My cousin Ron told me a story about how our fathers differed when it came to what to plant on the family farm. Dad wanted to try new vegetable crops that he had studied at college while Uncle Bruce insisted on the traditional cotton and wheat. Both brothers felt so strongly that their argument turned into a fistfight that moved outside, lasting until their father broke it up. As Ron rightly noted, his father would have won that fight; Uncle Bruce was bigger and stronger. But I loved that Dad took him on anyway, for the sake of doing something different.

Dad had a penchant for bringing home surprises—unexpected and unusual gifts. In the early 1960s, all phones were rotary, most a dull black, although Princess phones had just appeared on the market and some of my lucky girlfriends had them in their rooms. One day Dad arrived home with two most unusual phones. They were each one piece with the rotary dial on the bottom, shaped like an elongated handset. The style was notable but the colors stunning—bright yellow and red. The rumor was they were illegal, but that just contributed to the allure. I loved those phones and showed them off to friends, as did my brothers.

While other friends were getting their first car, often a discarded one from their parents or a farm's oldest pickup, my father found a white Anglia, a squarish British car about the size of a Volkswagen Bug, with gears that sounded like an approaching race car. It could barely hold four teenagers. Today, the car is familiar to fans of the Harry Potter movie series as it is the flying car. What the Anglia was doing on the High Plains of Texas I don't know, and how Dad found it was equally perplexing. In retrospect, it was another example of Dad being different, open to new ideas and things, willing to take a risk on a used car far away from any dealership. He was confident things would work out, a trait I've needed years to develop and one I never linked to Dad until this journey.

One Christmas Dad bought a large art print for Mom. It was of a young woman in the foreground and a young man a distance behind her, both attractive, both looking out from the painting with pensive eyes. In the background was a desert scene, with a rectangular pond just behind the woman. The colors were bright and the subject mystifying. I don't know what drew Dad to that picture, but it was the first piece of more modern art in our home and the only one in any of the homes I visited regularly, where pretty landscapes and still life paintings dominated the walls. It was different.

An uncle of mine once told me I was different. I only remembered that incident after Aunt Winnie shared her impressions of Dad, startling me with

CHARLES WALKER
Plainview
Agriculture

My father's college photo from Texas Tech.

the same adjective. The details of that conversation with my uncle elude me, despite efforts to recall the reasons for his observation. What I remember is not being surprised at the time by his comment. I always felt different, beginning in kindergarten when I colored an entire picture red because it was my favorite color. I didn't just color the little girl's dress red. I filled every nook and cranny of the picture with red. Teachers today would probably be concerned. My cousin was. I just thought it beautiful and fiercely resisted any suggestion of more colors. I knew it was different, but I didn't care.

My clothes were also always just a little off. Jumpers had a strange hold on me and I sought them out. I have needed glasses since third grade and I always chose the "different style" regardless of whether the selection was appropriate for my face. In high school, I had two pairs of shoes, one red and the other a dark chartreuse, unlike the standard black, brown or blue ones worn by most girls.

I spent a lot of time in my room with an imaginary life, sealed off from the rest of the house's chaos by a sliding door. There I listened to music, accepted the Olympic gold medal for gymnastics, was singled out to meet the Beatles and left behind the narrow world of Plainview for London or New York. Much of my pining for recognition was typical of adolescence, but I had a strong imagination based on extensive reading, and I was certain that my future would be outside the Texas Panhandle. Learning of Dad's early dreams of flying from my Aunt Winnie made me feel more normal, finally understanding that my way of viewing life's options had a genetic component.

Dad's dream of flying did come true. After getting his pilot's license in college, he never stopped flying. First, World War II put him in the pilot's seat of large cargo airplanes. Then, after returning home, he always had a plane, even if it was a small crop duster. He was able to use the plane in his work and to ferry his family around. He always seemed happy to climb into the cockpit.

My dreams were more nebulous and unformed. I wanted to see the world, yet with no specific plan or place in mind. My Aunt Helen was the first person I knew to travel abroad, and she brought me a typical doll for each country she visited. I kept my collection of dolls close, often wondering about their country of origin. Our trips in the summer prepared me for spending time in big cities and traveling long distances. My future held much more ambitious destinations and experiences that I began to accumulate as my confidence grew. The predictable sights of Europe gave way to paddling a canoe in the headwaters of the Amazon in Ecuador, riding an elephant in India, swimming in a darkened cave in Guatemala, hiking in Bhutan. After finding photos of Dad in Africa and India holding monkeys or hunting a gazelle, I felt a connection with his different experiences abroad. He would have loved mine.

My father's confidence and lack of fear were also notably different. I would observe my father during a tornado watch, remaining above ground as the rest of the family waited in our basement, scouting out the movement of the wind and rain, ready to dart to the cellar if necessary. I have never scared easily, and I can now attribute that, in part, to my father's calm nature under stress.

I can also see my father's confidence playing out in his life: starting a produce shed, buying an ice company, planting different crops, considering starting a vineyard, investing in coins with a friend. If he worried about all the balls he was juggling in the air, he didn't talk about it. My need for new ideas has played out in my traveling but also in more mundane ways, such as trying out new ethnic recipes on a regular basis, seeking out foreign films and hosting small dinner parties for good discussions. Even becoming a lawyer was something different and, at the time, still unusual for a woman—the biggest risk I've taken.

A previously unacknowledged connection with my father came with the realization that he loved history as much as I do. I read constantly growing up. Biographies were an early love—an introduction to history. Every summer Mom would take us to the old library downtown. It was

My father reading in his quiet time during the war. Photos of his father and mother are on the back shelf.

not air-conditioned, cooled instead with large overhead fans. I began with fiction—the Bobbsey Twins, followed by Nancy Drew—and continued with nonfiction. At school, dark silhouettes of the heads of historical figures adorned the outside cover of each biographical book at the back of College Hill Elementary's classrooms—Lincoln, Washington, Edison, Clara Mae Barton, Susan B. Anthony. I read through one or two a week. It was only after I started the search for Dad that I realized my father and I shared an interest in the past. He didn't have time to read books, but he did read newspapers and Newsweek. And when we vacationed, Dad was the last out of every museum we visited. He wanted to see and read it all.

My father and I never talked about our shared interest in history as we learned about the world on parallel paths. I now know how much he could have contributed to any discussion from his World War II world travels—descriptions of everyday life in Africa, India and China, how it felt to ride an elephant or befriend a monkey, the effect of the Hindu gods on the Indian people. Living right there in my home was a man whose life experiences far exceeded those of any other person I then knew, and I was clueless. I was learning from books, not realizing that Dad was a closed book that needed opening. Today, I want to reach back in time, shake him, make him talk, make him see me as a fellow traveler, bend his path to cross mine, absorb his personal stories.

As I learned of common characteristics that my father and I shared, his loss became harder to bear. The shared genes brought us closer and yet triggered frustration and a resentment at what I had lost. The "whys" that should have been asked fifty years ago surfaced. Why didn't he talk about his life? Why didn't he tell World War II stories? Where were the life lessons from starting a business? Where was the encouragement to follow my own different path? His early death was only one reason I couldn't know his answers to these questions. His regular absences and quiet nature compounded the loss. I would have to settle for what I discovered observing him, appreciating author Clarence Buddington Kellard's description of his father: "My father lived and let me watch him do it."

In high school, a single course lifted me from my small-town life on the dusty plains and dropped me into a world of philosophy, literature, architecture, drama and art: our senior-year humanities class, which had all the makings of a college course, with rotating teachers melding the arts of each era, beginning with the Greeks and continuing through the Middle Ages. We read Greek drama, analyzed Roman architecture, dissected Dante's "Inferno." For exams, I had to recognize slides of artworks, identify a quote or compare philosophies. My friends and I were so taken by the humanities course that we played games like Botticelli to challenge each other to guess a famous artist's name. We exchanged Christmas presents of philosophy books, even though we never read them. Add in the themes of four Shakespeare plays read over the four years of high school, and I was surprisingly ready for college, especially as the product of a small-town education system.

The humanities course gave me a confidence in my education and a sure footing in future college classes, an opportunity my father never had. I knew I had crossed a line with my awareness of the Western humanities tradition, a step up and beyond the boundaries of a farmer's daughter. Dad was gone by then, but I'm now certain that he would have been interested if I could have shared with him what I learned. He knew how it felt to step beyond boundaries, to embrace the outside world, to pursue a different path. My opportunity to do this was in the future; his was in the past. How sad they never crossed.

EIGHT

Thanksgiving and Christmas 1944

The World War II trunk revealed Dad's presence in Africa in more detail than I could have thought possible: holiday menus, his officer's card, photos from a hunt. More clues appeared with Dad's letter to Gene Rutledge. As well, I researched the route pilots flew across the Atlantic and learned of the dangers. A little investigation taught me that both the Gold Coast (now Ghana) and Nigeria were English possessions, which meant they were safe to use for World War II transportation purposes. Mont Jennings' letter helped with details about Misamari and Dad's final flight.

The puzzle pieces needed only a little glue to come together as letters I imagine Dad could have written his parents about his life abroad. While I'm sure any letters he wrote wouldn't have been as full of information as the ones I have created in this chapter and in Chapters 11, 14 and 16, I'm confident that they are true to his experience.

* * *

Maiduguri, Nigeria
December 25, 1944

Dear Mom and Dad,
Today is Christmas 1944, my first away from home. Last year I

would never have imagined I would be halfway around the world for this Christmas holiday, completely separated from you and my familiar, predictable life on the farm. I'm missing our Christmas tree, the cold weather outside and even the harvested fields. Homesickness is new to me, brought on by this war that blew into our Texas home and scattered our farm family across the globe. Have you heard from Bruce or Preston? Last I heard Bruce was in England and Preston in South America somewhere. I sure would like to hear from them. Is Lucy still posted in San Francisco? It makes me sad to think of the two of you in Texas on the farm, seated around a diminished table, wondering where and how we are all doing. I want to assure you both that I am all right.

I'm in Maiduguri, Nigeria, my second stop across the waist of Africa. I've been here all month, transporting men and supplies. My journey to Africa began in Nashville where I was assigned a ship (what we call planes) to fly overseas to India. Mine was a C-47, the workhorse of the transport operation. The path was worthy of an adventure movie: from Nashville to Miami, and from Puerto Rico into Belem and Natal Macaw, Brazil, the jumping off point for Africa. Minimal time was spent at each stop, only enough to refuel and occasionally rest.

The tiny Ascension Island—1,400 miles from Brazil and 1,000 miles from the coast of Africa—provides the only solid land to refuel in the entire Atlantic Ocean, a mere speck in the miles of water. It is nicknamed the "Widow's Pension": If you miss Ascension, your wife gets a pension. But if you stay on your dead reckoning route, radio beacons appear and the ground crew shoots the sun your way until you arrive on the correct longitude. Those who miss eventually run out of gas and crash. It was my first real challenge at flying without a safety net. My copilot and I exchanged growing-up stories to pass the time and calm our nerves. I know you're glad we were one of the lucky ones to find the island.

The Germans have been run out of northern Africa and many of the planes are now routed through Morocco, Tunisia and Egypt. I wasn't. I landed in Accra, capital of the Gold Coast, in October to help transport more troops and cargo. The Gold Coast is a surprising player in the World War II effort, as its factories assemble fighter and light aircraft for the Allies, and it has been a stopping point for the middle Africa transport route.

America's Thanksgiving holiday is unique in the world, and even in the Gold Coast the Army made sure we had a taste of home. You would have been so surprised at the spread provided—cream of celery soup; roast Vermont tom turkey; cranberry sauce; nut dressing; giblet gravy; whipped potatoes; butter string beans; boiled onions; cucumber, onion and tomato salad; olives; pickles; hot rolls and butter; pumpkin pie; and assorted fresh fruit, candy and mixed nuts. The pumpkin pie didn't compare to yours, Mom. White wine and American beer weren't listed but were served, a welcome surprise. I don't know what transport planes brought this feast into the country, but the commissary was full of grateful men who were transported to Thanksgivings past by the familiar taste and smell of the dishes. It was my first Thanksgiving abroad, and I realized that the importance of the holiday is to be surrounded by your family. My family has simply changed with the war to a diverse group of servicemen, stationed here by orders issued from above, connected by culture and language. I liked that.

Soon after Thanksgiving, I moved to Maiduguri, Nigeria, a base in the northern part of the country that sits on the Ngadda River. It is a peaceful town, filled with tree-lined streets and the Palace of the Bormis Sheikh that houses a beautiful mosque. Horses are used for transportation in the area, including for our officers, and a jeep checks out the runway before every flight to be sure camels haven't wandered on.

While I know we have a few Negroes back home in the Panhandle, I have never been around blacks in large numbers or with such dark skin. They are friendly and eager to help, seemingly oblivious to the hot, muggy temperatures. We buy oranges and other fruit from them alongside the main roads.

In between flying duties, I've checked out the agriculture and wildlife of the area. Peanuts are grown for export, harvested in sacks and stacked in pyramids—all by hand. I saw no tractors and no trace of the mechanization we use at home. Dad, we are lucky to have what we do for our farming.

From other soldiers, I learned of some hunting opportunities.

Thanksgiving Day menu in Gold Coast, Africa, 1944.

Since this time of the year at home we would be hunting dove and pheasants, I welcomed a chance to take down something different. I had no shotgun or hunting rifle, but the natives assured me that I could kill a gazelle with a pistol. They were right. Early one morning, two young Nigerians led me to a thorn thicket outside the base near an open stream to await the approach of animals of all kinds. A troop of monkeys came for their morning drinks, scattering a flock of green pigeons. A mother deer and her baby slowly entered the water, the baby spraying his mom. One of my guides quietly pointed to the tall grasses moving as a herd of gazelle hurried toward the stream, their horns visible above the grass line. They came close—maybe only 20 yards away—in an open area. My gun was ready. A smaller gazelle, grazing, approached our hiding place, unaware of our presence. The natives both nodded and I shot, instantly killing the beast and scattering the herd. A quick photo was taken of the catch with my camera by one of my guides, horns to the top. The animal was slender and weighed less than I expected, one reason they are so swift. It was a unique experience, one to share when I return home. Truthfully, the war seems far away.

Soon after I arrived, Richard Vickrey, a student of mine from 42-H in Uvalde, came through on his way to India with one of those B-29s. I was sure glad to see him, for he was the first student I had seen in a long time. We kidded around about our "hedgeshaping" the last day of instruction, when we flew so low to the ground that we could almost trim the bushes. We also caught up on other students. Vickrey was special. When he wrote me, he always complimented my teaching ability and he wanted me to be a part of his unit. Maybe I'll run into him again in India.

Now it's Christmas, probably the most unique one I'll ever experience. It's hot and humid outside. I've seen a few Anglican churches, but certainly no Southern Baptist ones like at home. Mainly it's a Muslim area, with calls to prayer throughout the day. Last night was a Christmas Eve candlelight service for the Protestants. Catholics got their own. We got to sing the familiar carols—"Silent Night," "Hark the Herald Angels Sing," "Oh Come, All Ye Faithful" and, at the end, "Joy to the World." Don't laugh but even I sang with my off-key voice. A good Christmas message by Chaplain Ketchum encouraged us to see the light at the end, especially appropriate in this time of war. And I had never really considered the words of "I Heard the Bells on Christmas Day." Three stanzas were printed in the service bulletin and the last one rang true.

Then pealed the bells more loud and deep;
God is not dead, nor doth he sleep,
The wrong shall fail, the right prevail,
Of peace on earth, good will to men.

At Christmas dinner Captain Lenz thanked us for carrying out our duties at this post—an easy one, I'm thinking. The meal was just as good as Thanksgiving's with roast "United States" turkey, lobster a la Newburg (a new one for me) and Georgia yams, Iowa corn and Montana string beans. Someone had fun with the menu names, although there was nothing from Texas. I had trouble choosing among the five desserts but finally picked the apple pie a la mode—again, not as good as yours, Mom. No beer or wine this time.

There were 20 of us around a long table and someone decided we should sign each other's menus, a confirmation of our presence at this time and place. I didn't really know any of the soldiers well, but I started signing as each menu was passed to the right. I may never see any of them again, but our signatures confirmed we shared a Christmas meal together in the middle of a war on a continent none of us ever expected to see. I savored the moment, knowing what was ahead of me.

My order to report to India to fly the Hump just came in. The landscape is about to dramatically change and wartime about to get real. But don't worry. I'll be fine. I've had good training. I'll write you more about it when I get there.

Until then, Merry Christmas and Happy New Year.

Love,

Charlie

NINE

Surveying the Crops

It is a bright, hot summer afternoon, perfect growing weather for the potato, cabbage and onion crops on our farm. The cotton fields also bask in the warmth. On Sundays Dad loves to show off his crops. While other friends take trips to parks or the movies, go waterskiing or fishing, or play with neighborhood kids, we drive to the farm to "survey the crops," as my mother calls it. Mom is not a farm-wife type and was happy when we moved into town, with neighbors, schools and stores nearby. But since we now live in town, Dad wants to be sure we know where we come from, what our livelihood depends on, what a beautiful crop looks like.

On this day we drive along the dirt roads through and around our farm, Dad keeping an eye out for any stray weeds that need to be chopped off. He stops to check on an irrigation ditch that brings water to the fields from the underground aquifer. Not satisfied with the flow, Dad jumps out and insists we get out too. Not for the first time, he demonstrates how to create a vacuum in an irrigation pipe and push it quickly into a row of cotton. Gary gets the nod to start the water flow for the next row. He does, we applaud and I'm grateful to be passed over.

We pull up to the "hired hands'" homes on our property. Dad has two families living on our farm. The houses are small, basic two-bedroom structures, built of adobe, painted and solidly built. The children are outside, playing in the dirt yards. As he often does, Dad stops to visit, joking around with the kids, waiting for a child to run inside to advise their parents of our presence. Soon, they come out to talk.

The fathers of the two families seem happy to see him and listen as Dad talks farm talk with them. Unlike many migrant workers that pass quickly through our area, one family has lived here for several years. The second family has been on our farm for only a few months and will probably move on in the fall. Soon, we kids are out of the car, my younger brothers shyly approaching the other children to play. Mom smiles at their wives. Since none of us speaks Spanish, a language barrier prevents much detailed communication. One boy from the newer family is about my age and I recognize him from my fourth grade class last semester. I didn't realize his father worked for mine. We have never spoken in class and I'm not sure how to begin a conversation now. After a while, Dad turns to leave, we say our goodbyes and return to our home in town.

* * *

A S WITH SO many of my recovered memories of Dad, I can now layer a mature level of experience over the original picture to see the nuanced movements of the players. In the farm scene, there was something about my father's approach to his employees that reflected his respect for the work they did—his willingness to stop, the gentle banter, the relaxed stance. I can also see the mutual respect in the workers' relationship with him—direct eye contact, straight backs, easy smiles. They knew nobody worked harder than Dad. It was a rare mingling of our families, but one my parents were comfortable with.

Migrant children appeared in my elementary school in the fall as their parents moved north to help with the harvest. The public-school class at College Hill Elementary reflected the makeup of the Texas Panhandle. Farmers, professionals, teachers, business owners, office workers and bankers' children were white and dominant. Children of the farmhands, domestics and line workers for agricultural processing were brown and a minority. Missing from the class was any representation of the small black community; they had their own segregated school, Booker T. Washington.

I remember one painful calling-out of Hispanic students. My fourth-grade teacher used test scores to arrange our seating. If you did well on the exam, you sat in the first row for that week. Those in the fourth row had scored the lowest, a kind of public shaming that was condoned. The last ones to be called would quickly find their seats, heads ducked, shoulders slumped, avoiding eye contact with the rest of the class. They were mostly boys, mostly Hispanics and possibly migrants.

With no ESL support, migrant children had a double challenge to score high on those fourth-grade tests. It was sink-or-swim for them in the all-English class. They remained part of our school until their families returned south. I was familiar with the pattern, as my father hired the temporary workers, both to help with the harvest of vegetables and cotton and to work on the noisy conveyor belt at our produce shed, moving the harvest along to be washed, sorted and bagged for sale.

The children in the fourth row may have been from migrant parents that worked for my Dad, but I never thought to ask. And while I noted the difference in grade results, I wasn't mature enough or even sensitive enough to recognize the economic and language conditions being played out in the classroom.

To manage our produce shed, Dad hired Mario Trevino, a large man with a big smile. Mario did all the translating and helped run the increasingly hectic office. Race apparently was not an issue for my father in hiring. He wanted the best person in the position. Mario was always at the shed when we came to visit. Our families exchanged Christmas gifts. He had only one daughter, who had health problems. Mom would always inquire about her and about his wife. When my father died, Mario was one of the most devastated. He couldn't see any of us children without tearing up.

I can't remember Dad saying anything racially negative about his crew or staff. Maybe he did in private or around other men. But at home he and Mom were modeling how to treat those who were different. No slang words were used in our house to describe Hispanics, although my mother would call them "the Spanish," a term I heard nowhere else—Mom's attempt at being politically correct. The common description back then was "Mexicans." My grandparents weren't above using the "N word" for blacks, but not my parents. Maybe, from his childhood, my father knew how it felt to do the physical work of farming, and he respected the workers. Maybe his consciousness had been raised during his travels through Africa and Asia, where a mix of races did fine as a majority in their own lands. Maybe my mother had experienced too many of her own tragedies and could relate to theirs. I just know that I looked on those students

My father proudly posing with boxes of lettuce featuring his brand name, "Plains Gold."

in the fourth row with sadness not with hate or superiority, and I have my parents to thank for that.

The memories of the Sunday drives to the farm were important in another way, after my father died, when they stopped. After I left home for college, Sunday afternoons were always hard for me. Seldom did I have anything special to do except needing to discipline myself to study or prepare for the week, but without the focus or energy to do so. I was most homesick on those days, calling my mother to hear her voice, sometimes feeling worse after hanging up. Even in my working life, a sadness and weight often appeared on Sundays, accompanying me until the next morning. Only in remembering those Sunday drives to the farm have I realized that I missed those excursions to our land, to the connection with our family's livelihood, to the strength of the earth and underground water, to the silence as the crops slowly revealed their internal beauty. Our Sunday visits provided reassurance that life would go on, that the cycle never finished, that hope was always there for the finished crop. Life did go on after Dad died, but it was never the same.

TEN

Flying the Hump:
The Family Myth

Growing up in the Texas Panhandle introduced my father to storms so severe that they intimidated natives as much as they did visitors. Tornadoes in the spring played chess with towns and farms, taking down homes and equipment in a haphazard manner, leaving those untouched feeling simply lucky. Freezes from late storms in the spring and early ones in the fall destroyed crops and a family's hope for a profitable year.

I remember the sinking feeling I always had when a hailstorm hit in the Texas Panhandle, hoping our new plants weren't victims. Dad knew how capricious and strong weather could be, but nothing in Texas could prepare him for a Himalayan storm, the terror of all pilots flying the Hump.

* * *

I DON'T REMEMBER the first time I discovered Dad had flown the Hump in World War II. Certainly, he didn't tell me. He never shared a word about those experiences and I never asked. I did know, somehow, that Dad was respected for his part in flying the Hump. I knew it was considered risky flying and that the Himalayas were involved, as was India and China.

Despite the lack of details, his story was always a presence in our family—hazy, nebulous with a ring of excitement, meritorious in military parlance, comparable to those who saw combat, superior to those who served in noncombat positions. A mythical quality surrounded his postings in India and China, exotic and distant places. Our home decor reflected some of his experiences abroad: knives from Africa, a water pipe from China, a brass mosaic vase from India that rested on our bookcase for years…small, silent tokens that could have told parts of his story.

The Hump experience carried over into Dad's demeanor in everyday life. As described by a contemporary of his, my father always wore an air of competence and authority, but with warmth—possibly from working with pilots and others as a team in dangerous situations and from being responsible for the missions. I noted that adults reacted with respect if his war years came up. But when quizzed as an adult, I couldn't contribute any anecdotal events, only a brief summary of the operation. It is embarrassing to realize how ignorant I was, even while being proud of his accomplishment. Only in exploring the Hump's history have I finally learned how very proud we should have been.

Flying the Hump was the moniker given to the airlift operation in World War II that brought supplies, primarily gasoline, from India to Chiang Kai-shek and US General Joseph Stillwell in western China. The Japanese occupied all of eastern China and had turned around the southeastern curve of Asia, gobbling up modern-day Vietnam, Cambodia and Thailand and threatening Burma. President Roosevelt wanted to keep China in the war because if China could hold the line against the Japanese western advance, then Japan would have to fight on two fronts.

After the Japanese blocked all Pacific ports into China, the Burma Road was built to supply western China. When the Japanese invaded lower Burma and had easy access to bombing the road, it was closed. President Roosevelt insisted on finding an alternative method to get high-octane fuel into China, for both Stillwell and the Chinese army. The Hump route was an unlikely path for regular flight operations due to high terrain and extremely severe weather. It crossed a north-south extension of the main Himalaya mountains that runs south through western China and northern Burma. At the very north end of the extension, terrain rises to more than twenty thousand feet. Average elevations are lower to the south, though they never fall below twelve thousand feet. The routes flown by Hump pilots like my father ranged between these two extremes.

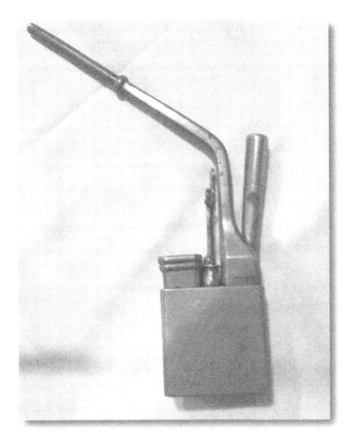

Water pipe that my father brought home.

In 1942 only one airfield—in Dinjan, India—was usable for the operation. Over the next three years, about twenty-five more landing strips would be built, including in Misamari where my father would be posted. British tea-plantation owners were "encouraged" to allow bases to be built on their land, and the local population was put to work constructing steel runways that were surrounded by tea plants.

Most supplies for the airlift originated in the US. They were shipped by sea to Calcutta (now Kolkata) and brought in over a narrow-gauge railroad to the Assam Valley, taking weeks to finally arrive. While the Hump operation concentrated on gasoline, all weapons, machinery, repair parts, troops, and even whiskey had to be transported first by sea and plane.

The hesitancy to use the Hump as a major supply route was well-founded, its danger borne out by the statistics. There was an average of two accidents for every thousand hours flown, and a plane went down for every two hundred trips over the mountains. For every thousand tons flown into China, three Americans gave their lives. The perils were many.

Early in the war, Japanese fighter pilots operating out of Burma would appear, forcing Hump planes to clumsily attempt an escape while avoiding mountaintops. Despite their mission's description as a transport operation, Hump pilots faced real aerial combat, but without the ability to fight back—adding to its reputation as a hazardous post. In the early months after my father's arrival in 1945, the Japanese retreated from Burma, eliminating one of the flying hazards he had originally faced.

More than any factor, the battle against Himalayan weather challenged the success of the Hump operation. Weather forecasting was a problem from the beginning. Most storms originated in the Soviet Union, which routinely ignored requests for ground conditions. China's forecast information was sketchy and unreliable. Even US weathermen, trained in cold fronts passing over our country, were unfamiliar with the trajectory of Asian storms. Information shared by pilots crossing the Hump with each other would have been the most helpful for my father, but conditions could have changed completely by the time Dad got into the cockpit.

A deadly mix of weather patterns hung out over the Himalayan route. Freezing air movement from Siberia met warm, wet tropical pressure from the Bay of Bengal. The result was a cold Asiatic air mass blasting across the Himalayas, mixing with the mountains' frigid temperatures and with warm moisture from the south, causing snow and the dreaded ice. The only deicing mechanisms available were wipers that brushed ice from wings, activated by pilots desperate to lighten their plane's load. Without successful removal of ice, planes lost altitude and speed, a potentially deadly combination when skimming the top of the world's highest mountains overloaded with barrels of gasoline.

The capricious wind and its updrafts were completely new to the war's young pilots. They were much more powerful than the relatively tame turbulence that modern-day commercial pilots consider serious enough to activate the alert that directs passengers to be sure their seatbelts are securely fastened and attendants to take a seat. Even my father's training in the mountains near Reno, Nevada couldn't prepare him for the hundred-mile-an-hour blasts that jerked a plane four to five thousand feet on the updraft of a mountain ridge and then slammed it back down on the valley side, sometimes even flipping the plane over. Pilots were helpless to intervene until beyond a draft, by which time they were often disoriented by the sudden movements that could ensue amid near-zero visibility. My only experience with a real air pocket occurred in a nighttime thunderstorm high over the Andes mountains on the way to Ecuador several years ago with Ecuatoriana Airlines. It was sudden and frightening, and it caused all kinds of prayers to be moaned and shouted around the cabin. Yet the drop was over quickly and wouldn't have compared to the punches and kicks that Dad's planes received over the Himalayas.

Compounding the challenge of the wind was rain. The Assam Valley is one of the wettest places on earth, getting 120 inches of rain or more a year. During the monsoon season that extends from June through September, heavy rains would have been a constant presence. Immediately after takeoff and until landing, pilots had to rely on instruments, often spotting the runway only in the final seconds before landing. And with constant cloud cover, thunderstorms couldn't always be seen or anticipated.

Since my father was in Africa in December 1944, it is doubtful that he would have been in India in time to fly on January 6 and 7, 1945, a twenty-four-hour period known as "Black Friday." Those who flew then encountered the worst weather of the operation. Winds were directly out of the north-northwest at a hundred miles an hour, forcing pilots and navigators to make significant course-corrections. Airspeeds raced from 80 to 260 mph and back as gusts flung planes up and down at rates of four thousand feet per minute. Ice coated the planes. Maydays were received from pilots reporting lost engines or desperately trying to discover where they had been tossed. Some pilots advised anyone who was listening on the radio that they were bailing out. When the storm ended, eighteen planes had been lost, along with forty-two crewmen and passengers, the deadliest loss of the Hump operation.

Even if my father didn't fly that night, he would have heard about it, surely increasing his anxiety about joining the Hump operation. He would also have known that planes had to fly—in clear, rainy, icy or windy weather. Because of the terrain, the weather and the pressure to fly at all times, Dad's route to China from India along the Able route—over twelve- to twenty-thousand-foot mountains—was considered the most hazardous regularly used air lane in the world. My father would soon fly that route 150 times.

ELEVEN

Passing through Karachi, India

This is the second letter I "constructed" from my research, this one based on an unexpected reunion that Dad had with a Plainview friend—a real event that I learned about from a photo I found with Dad's writing on the back.

* * *

January 1945

Dear Mom and Dad,

I'm headed to the Assam Valley in eastern India to fly the Hump from Misamari, India to Kunming, China. You may not be familiar with this assignment but stories of flying the Hump route have filtered down to me as I get closer, expanded by more returning pilots: basic barracks, flying duties every other day, treacherous weather, the occasional need to bail out with a parachute into dense jungle below. My planes will be carrying gasoline to the Chinese and Americans in western China. That's what I have to look forward to. When I was training in the Nevada mountains, instructors tried to prepare us for mountain flying, with its updrafts and downdrafts, constant instrument flying in the clouds, and snow and ice on the wings. They knew the terrain didn't compare to the revered and feared Himalayas, but it was an introduction. Their advice seems remote today in Karachi, a steaming hellhole in India even in January, where I just got that next assignment to Misamari.

All transient aircraft headed east must pass through here. The Allied base at Karachi is busy with supplies moving eastward from Iran and departing for various destinations in India. Planes and crew members move in both directions.

You're not going to believe this coincidence. After checking in, I found the Officers Club, an appreciated reprieve from war duties and a guaranteed place to exchange stories. I ordered a beer and moved to an open table, knowing other GIs would join me.

Soon a familiar voice asks, "Mind if I join you?" I feel a hand on my shoulder. Looking up, I see Leighton Maggard, my old friend from Plainview! It's the second time I have run into him, the first being in Cairo. He's now stationed in Karachi as a flight operations officer.

It was so exciting to connect with someone from home. Unexpectedly meeting a friend on the other side of the world seems to lighten the conversation. Leighton and I talked easily, reminiscing about our people, sharing what little gossip we had from home, comparing our war stories. It was a welcome experience in a world where every view, encounter, food and belief is new.

Leighton gave me a hard time about moving on to India to fly the Hump, remarking on my bad luck. He'd heard the same stories I had about the horrible weather and difficult flying conditions. I laughed with him, keeping my anxiety to myself. But Mom and Dad, please know I am ready to make that first flight over those big mountains the pilots call the Rockpile, even a little excited—confident of my training and flying ability.

Next stop is Agra, India, home of the Taj Mahal. We're promised time to do a little sightseeing before heading to Misamari and I'm looking forward to seeing that famous mausoleum and maybe having some time to shop for souvenirs. It will be my last respite until I get enough flying hours in over the Hump to qualify for some R&R.

Please tell the Maggards that I saw Leighton and he looked good.

Love,

Charlie

TWELVE

A Quiet Father

The Plainview High School band always marches in the rodeo parade and 1965 is no exception. As a twirler, I am out front, twisting and tossing my baton to the music, trying to stay in line with the other twirlers. It's hot today, especially compared to the fall temperature we are used to marching in. But the routine is simple and the crowd friendly.

As we march across Fifth Street, I see my father in his new, white Plymouth Sports Fury, waiting in the line of cars for the parade to pass. He must be on his way to the farm from the produce shed. The parade ends soon after that intersection, and I run to his car to ask for a ride home. It's not much out of the way. He agrees and I hop in.

I love the new car, with its bucket seats and low ride. My bare legs gently touch the warm leather interior. Hopefully, some of my friends will see me in it.

Dad smiles as I get in but says nothing. We don't talk all the way home. It's not an uncomfortable silence. Dad is often distracted, retreating into an active silence, his eyes giving him away—distant but engaged. He is lost in thought today, probably some business matter weighing on him. I'm used to his taciturn nature around the kids, although I notice he easily talks to his male friends. Maybe he just doesn't have much to say to his children. When we get to the house, I exit, thank him for the ride and he quickly drives off.

* * *

I THINK BACK on that day and realize that Dad's voice eludes me. How did I know it was him when he called home to prepare Mom for his late arrival? I recall softness not harshness in a voice never raised, even when he disciplined us. But the timbre is missing. Would I even recognize it if he called today? Our home movies show the man but not the voice.

I can't even remember anything Dad ever said to me—no sayings, no teasing, nothing. Mom had her phrases: "Oh my goodness," good grief," "For heaven's sake" and an occasional "Hell's bells," as close to an expletive as she got with her children. I'm sure Dad had stock sayings for frustration or wonder, yet they simply won't surface. After he served in World War II, I would guess that he had some private curses, but he didn't use them in front of the kids.

There are also no remembered words of advice that might have yielded insight into starting my own business, spreading my wings, facing new challenges, risk-taking as a part of life. He didn't impart wisdom for dealing with setbacks. Looking at all his businesses, I know he must have had them. That doesn't mean I didn't learn from him. While there were no words of wisdom, he made no negative comments. There was no belittling from Dad. He never tore down our self-esteem. There were no sighs of disappointment. I didn't recognize this as a gift until hearing friends' stories of fathers who were mean or who demeaned their children. It's the absence of negative words that was really a positive. Silence converted into active modeling. I want his words, but I must be content with his quiet parenting style, learning more from what he did and didn't do than what he said.

Thinking back, I wonder what I would have done had he turned to me in the car after the parade and asked about my day. The inquiry would have been startling, an unexpected interest in my life, an intrusion into our normally silent encounters. Would I have answered with a shrug? Would I have been struck mute by the unusual eye contact, falling deeper into the leather seats and into a teenager's refusal to share feelings or information? Or maybe the time would have been right to blurt out my agony over a guy who liked me but whom I didn't like and ask Dad, as a sudden car counselor, to give me advice on how to get out of the relationship with minimal embarrassment. Would Dad with sage words acknowledge my pain, compliment my looks and smarts, and send me out with newfound confidence? None of this seems likely, but I do know the sudden dip into my life's details would have been appreciated and maybe, just maybe, I would now be able to remember something he said.

Another fair question is, what he would have done if I had inquired that day about his World War II experience? How interested would I have been in the details of his life in India or in the challenges faced by pilots over the Himalayas? Could I have been pulled out of my myopic teenage life long enough to understand how incredible his war years had been? Looking back over the scene today, I see the opportunity to draw Dad out after a parade full of patriotic flags, but I also see a fifteen-year-old teenager who, like her friends, didn't have a clue how to start that kind of conversation with a forty-seven-year-old father. It was a missed opportunity for me and for him, one that should have orbited back around as we both aged but didn't because of his early death.

THIRTEEN

The Revered C-47: A Workhorse of the Hump Operation

After returning to the States from our trip to India and China, I meet my brother in Plainview for a reunion. Mack picks me up at the Lubbock airport. He has a surprise for me. We drive to the original Lubbock terminal where we used to fly with Dad on slow summer afternoons to get a Coca-Cola. It is now a war museum concentrating on the gliding training that took place there during World War II. In the circle in front of the building is a solitary plane.

"Do you recognize it?" Mack asks, grinning. I do. It is a C-47, the very model Dad was flying on his last flight with Mont Jennings and probably the one he would have flown often over the Himalayas.

The plane seems lonely there, put out to pasture, possibly wondering where all those pilots went who use to call her "Gooney Bird," missing the incredible action that came its way during World War II. The nose of the plane points up, pushing the cockpit high overhead. Seven small windows line each side; troops would have peered down out of them to the snow-covered mountains below. The cargo door is closed, masking the plane's ability to load a fully constructed jeep or twenty-four barrels of gasoline. Two prop engines stand ready to roar into action, even in the densest rain.

I picture Dad climbing up the ramp and in through the side door, moving forward to the cockpit. This is the machine he would have flown to do battle with the elements, to carry needed fuel and to follow orders to fly day and night. This is the machine that would have kept him safe. Basic, simple, strong, ready to fly, then fly some more. A plane that did its duty without complaint, like my father. For all those reasons, I love it.

* * *

ON THIS JOURNEY, I never expected to fall in love with a plane. When I first researched the aircraft that Dad would have flown over the Hump, the distinctions between the C-47 and other planes, such as the C-46, C-54 and B-29, were a blur—a mix of purposes and of statistics about size, horsepower and maneuverability. Gradually, however, they became distinct, each with its own merits and accomplishments. With each revealed usage of the C-47 plane, my admiration grew, developing into awe at its reliability and flexibility.

As a history buff, I loved its past. The C-47 was a wartime variant of the famous DC-3 that was first developed in 1935. The DC-3 has attained almost mythical status as the plane that introduced the American public to air transportation, able to cross the United States in 1938 in a record eighteen hours and forty minutes. Passengers on those early transcontinental flights were served meals on Syracuse china with Reed & Barton silverware, and they slept in berths with goose-down comforters. A mere four years later, with wartime modifications that included a reinforced floor for heavy cargo and engines designed for the thin air over the Himalayas, the DC-3 became the armed forces' C-47B.

I liked that the plane responded well to its pilots, keeping my father safe. The "Gooney Bird," as pilots fondly called it, beginning in early 1942 when planes started flying the Hump from India to China. Pilots liked them. As one World War II Hump pilot described it, they were a dream to fly, almost taking off on their own and flying themselves. It was the required landing that was tricky. Many pilots noted that those planes preferred to keep on flying.

I admired the C-47's ability to fly on instruments, a much-needed feature for Hump pilots. A straight shot across in clear weather at high altitudes would have been hard enough, but many flights flew through deep

With C-47 at the Lubbock Airport, Texas.

clouds, directed only by those rudimentary instruments. Some pilots measured three-fourths of their flying time in the clouds. Dad had instrument training and was sent to Reno for exposure to mountain flying. Because of his years of flying experience, he probably felt he had an advantage over other newly arrived pilots, but he still had a lot of learning to do.

Some instruments were particularly important after most takeoffs in India when Dad's plane would disappear into a dense cloud of moisture, leaving him with no visual cues. He would need the altimeter and other instruments to obey the control tower when it ordered him to ascend or descend in the five-hundred-foot increments required to avoid a midair crash, especially in cloud-covered conditions. Also, without radar, all a pilot had to guide him along the correct flight path was a pointer on the instrument panel that spun when the plane crossed a radio beacon that had been placed on the ground for navigation purposes. Japanese troops were known to move beacons to confuse Allied pilots, adding to the constant worry. Dad's extensive wartime experience with instrument flying explains his later comfort in flying in inclement weather at home, in storm conditions that other pilots would have waited out on the ground.

I loved the C-47's versatility. While carrying cargo was its primary function, the plane also generously offered its services to search for accidents and crew bailouts, to pull gliders with people and supplies behind enemy lines, to carry bombs, to serve on weather-reconnaissance detail, and, on occasion, to engage in direct warfare, with pilots and crew members firing pistols out windows and open doors at attacking Japanese planes. Even

General Eisenhower recognized the C-47 as an important contributor to victory in World War II.

As I learned more about the plane, I became aware of some of the challenges that pilots like my father faced. In the first C-47s, no heat was available in the cockpit, and oxygen was always required because the plane was not pressurized. The oxygen masks were uncomfortable and made communication difficult. A photo of a pilot in an oxygen mask with the Himalayas in the background surfaced in some old photos, surprising me with how large the masks were. As well, ice on the wings was a constant threat and could only be swept away by wipers or melted by descending thousands of feet.

Dad with crew member in front of their C-46. I do not have a photo of my father in front of a C-47.

Dad would have been familiar with two other wartime planes. In 1943 the C-46, younger brother to the C-47, showed up—affectionately called "Old Dumbo," "Commando" and, with black humor, "Flying Coffin." With its twin two-thousand-horsepower engines, this plane could cruise at 220 mph. Inside its enlarged, twenty-one-foot-cargo bay, trucks or artillery could be carried, and even more gasoline. Since Dad was checked out to fly both the C-47 and C-46, I'm sure he enjoyed the newer plane's "luxuries": a more comfortable cockpit, heat, solarium-like windows, seats with adjustable headrests, rudder pedals and an adjustable control column.

An even later addition to the Hump fleet was the C-54, a four-engine plane also known as the DC-4, which would later become the prototype for American commercial airlines. It was called the "general's plane" because it was the one selected to carry bigwigs into India and China. All Hump pilots dreamed of flying this relatively huge plane that carried three times the load of a C-47 and had a range of twenty-five hundred miles. We have one photo of Dad in front of a C-54, so I hope he got to fly one before leaving India.

I can't say that I became obsessed with the C-47, but I took every opportunity to quiz pilots and World War II aficionados about their knowledge of its accomplishments. World War II "fly-ins" to nearby airports that featured vintage planes became interesting for me to attend. And hanging on my office wall today is a framed, colored print of a painting by aviation artist Roy Grinnell, of a C-47 flying over the Himalayas on a dappled day. Despite dark clouds in the background, the sun is shining on the plane, projecting its shadow onto the snow-covered mountains below. It's titled "Over the Top of the World" and it feels like a family photo handed down from a father to his daughter.

There are still some C-47s flying in the world—mostly in developing countries, although I read about a few in Alaska. According to my brother, Gary, my family flew in a DC-3, possibly a former C-47, in 1973 from Quito, Ecuador to Guayaquil on the coast and he still remembers the spacious interior.

In addition to Mack's discovery in Lubbock, a friend, Stuart Dodson, told me about a C-47 at the Mid America Flight Museum in Mount Pleasant, Texas, just fifty miles from where I live. That C-47 was part of the D-Day invasion of Europe and has been meticulously restored. The interior is much smaller than I imagined it would be, increasing my marvel at its ability to transport so much cargo over the Himalayas.

The day of our visit to the museum coincided with the C-47's move from the back of a hanger out into the sunshine. To get the C-47 out, the smaller planes blocking it had to be first brought out of the hangar and parked on either side of the building's broad driveway. Finally, the big plane eased slowly forward, its pilot's cabin pointed high in the air, moving regally down the center aisle between the other planes, its large wingspan barely missing some of them. In that moment, I was as close as I would ever get to seeing Dad taxi his plane out to a wartime runway, a thrill even these seven decades later. The C-47 is an easy plane to love.

FOURTEEN

Arrival at the Base

THIS IMAGINED LETTER from my father comes primarily from information in the Mont Jennings interview.

* * *

Misamari, India
January 1945

Dear Mom and Dad,

I made it to the Assam Valley and am in a small Indian town that now hosts an American army base. Misamari is on the north side of the Brahmaputra, a huge river that runs through the valley. The base itself has been built on a tea plantation requisitioned from the owner. Lush tea bushes grow throughout the Assam Valley and up the hills. It was a beautiful sight flying in, so different from the flat farmland of the Texas Panhandle. The full green tea bushes reminded me of our mature cotton crops ready to harvest, but the bushes here are larger. I enjoyed my journey over, getting to see parts of Africa and the Middle East, flying above vast deserts, river valleys and deltas and lots of mountains. We got a little time off in Agra, and some pals and I went to see the beautiful Taj Mahal. The Indians sure did stare at us.

Here at the base, I've been assigned a bache, a 40-foot-long building divided in two—20 feet on each side, with three bunks in each half. It's pronounced BA-chee, or at least that's how we say it. Two walls are solid bamboo wood and the other two are screened in. A one-foot-thick thatch roof covers the structure, allowing only a fine mist to filter through during the many rainy days. For some reason, monkeys love to run across the roof at all hours. They are just as playful here as they were in Africa.

When I first met the barracks' bache boy, he smiled at me and in his English accent made me understand that his job is to take my gear out to dry when the sun is shining and to quickly return it inside when the rain begins. He is paid 8¢ a day. That seems like nothing, but it's double the salary paid by local tea-plantation owners, making him eager to please and the plantation owners angry. He wants to keep this job! With all the rain they get here, he should be busy dashing in and out of the baches during intermittent lulls. It's not like home, where our crops must be irrigated to maturity if the rains are insufficient. As a Texas boy, I like our sun and I fear the constant rain will be depressing.

When I first entered my bache, two pilots were asleep under their mosquito netting, resting before their night assignment or after the previous night's trip. A "quiet" sign hung outside the door. I tucked my gear under my bunk and decided to explore. The sun was out but the Himalayas were still covered in clouds, invisible despite being just four miles away. I really feel their presence, patiently waiting for me to challenge their peaks. The runway was nearby, made of mesh steel rather than paved asphalt, by now a standard for many of the bases built for the war effort. I've already discovered that the plane feels different pushing out over the mesh steel. Rougher and noisier.

You wouldn't be surprised that since I'm a High Plains boy, I always notice the wind. Here, the east-west wind up the valley parallels the runway. Because of the high Himalayas, north winds get deflected, at least until you're climbing to cruising altitude. We have a single control tower where controllers direct the steady stream of C-46s and C-47s taking off and landing. An occasional four engine C-54 makes an appearance. I watched the activity for a while, amazed at the constant landing and departing, ten minutes apart. Some planes were set to the side of the runway, parked for maintenance that's carried out at night, even in inclement weather. We were told we would fly in almost all weather conditions and every other day, at all hours. But we have good planes and good crews so I'm not worried and neither should you be.

From the base, I walked to Misamari's busy railroad station. That's where much of the gasoline for the planes comes in. The state of Assam has the only oil refinery in India, providing some of the gas. The rest is shipped into Calcutta and then sent on by river, rail or pipeline. My usual cargo will be those barrels of gasoline; they're needed by the American army and Chiang Kai-shek's Chinese army, mainly to keep their planes flying. Other pilots have warned us to use the barrels as ballast if a plane loses altitude too quickly in a storm. Simply roll them out the door and hope they fall harmlessly on the jungle below! I guess we will do what we have to do to stay aloft.

At the station I watched the locals maneuvering the barrels out of a railcar and onto a truck. They will have to be loaded onto the planes next. I heard that elephants have been trained to do this job, but none were at it this morning. But I saw some along the road to Misamari, several carrying logs out of a forest, my introduction to these huge beasts. I'm told wild elephants sometimes crash through the jungle near the base at night. The war effort has clearly swept up much of the Assam Valley in its operation, requiring many workers and animals.

On my way back to the barracks from my tour of the base, I passed a hospital, shower building and the doctors' houses. There are several of these spread throughout the plantation. When I first arrived, I had a very brief medical checkup that primarily consisted of advice on what to do if I had to bail out of the plane!! A dental technician then inspected my teeth in case I had to be identified by dental records—a sobering thought. Don't panic, Mom. This is just standard operating procedure. I'm also required to start taking Atabrine, a pill to ward off malaria. I can tell that some of the men have been here a while, as their skin has yellowed from the drug.

Well, I better close. It's getting dark and it looks like rain. My first flight is tomorrow morning, the initial round trip to Kunming and the beginning of my required 750 hours of flying before I can return home. I'm ready to challenge those hidden peaks, to see this operation in action, and ready to have my own stories.

Take care of yourselves. I know I will. Write if you can.

Love,

Charlie

Early 1945 at 1328th AFBU, Misamari. L/R: Back Row: Bud Jones (Syracuse, NY); Charles Walker, deceased (Plainview, TX); Frank Tate (State College MS); L/R, Front Row: Bob Lineberger (Lincolnton NC); Chris Mehiel (Brooklyn, NY); and Jim Bowie (Nashville, TN).

Newspaper article about my father's unit, the 1328th AFBU in Misamari, early 1945.

FIFTEEN

Late Discoveries in a Forgotten Box

When my mother died in early 2010, my brothers and I gathered around what was left of her personal affects. She had moved twice before settling into an assisted-living home in Albuquerque, and most of her furniture and personal memorabilia had been divided or sold in those transitions. Our time to divide what remained was limited, and the box of photos seemed overwhelming. Not knowing what the box contained, we assigned it to our youngest brother, Jeff, to sort out.

It's now eight years later and I'm visiting Jeff. I ask about the box, and he sheepishly admits to it still being unexplored. That evening we open it and examine its aged contents, just as I have done with every other hidden treasure on this journey—the World War II trunk, letters from students, the letter from Dad to my uncle, the letter containing his high school grades and now this box of photos…a past that keeps giving.

* * *

Small Gestures

I pulled out a photo of the seven of us, an unfamiliar one, taken during our summer trip to Washington and California in 1966. In the picture, we are in the backyard of a high school friend of my mother's, all dressed casually—the kids in jeans, Mom in slacks and my father in the khaki working pants he often wore. My two older brothers' hair had grown out some, but the other two brothers and my father had the burr haircut of the fifties.

Something was different about this picture and it took me a minute to identify it. It was Dad's arm: In the photo it's thrown around my shoulder, holding me close. The gesture was simple but unusual. And he's smiling broadly, as if happy to be at my side. I couldn't remember him doing that in any other picture. I couldn't remember him doing it at all. We weren't a physical family. When we were young, my brothers and I never threw an arm around a shoulder or a waist spontaneously unless we were wrestling. It made me happy to know Dad would do that, an indication of affection.

As I looked through more photos in the box, I noticed he did that in other family pictures too—holding Jeff's hand for an Easter portrait, a hand on Gary's shoulder in a Christmas card photo. He did it more often than Mom did.

My mother didn't start telling us regularly that she loved us until Dad was gone and her children were adults. My father didn't live long enough for us to mature and not be embarrassed to speak openly about our feelings. But those small gestures in the old photos spoke to me through time. I can't remember him ever saying he loved me but from the smile on his face, I felt he did. His love was subtle, but present.

Dad's Wallet

At the bottom of the box was a black Lord Buxton Convertible wallet, a bit worn and fanned open slightly from its bulging contents. I guessed immediately that it was my father's wallet, the one he would have been carrying the night he collapsed. In it would be evidence of what was important enough to him to carry close. It could tell a tale, provide a snapshot of his life at that moment in time, offer an unplanned personal history lesson for his children. As with each new discovery of my father, I paused then slowly opened the wallet as if I were about to read a long sought-after diary.

Tucked into the first three plastic sleeves were photos of each member of the family—Mom with me, then individual pictures of my four brothers and me. On the back of mine, I had written "to the greatest Dad in the world" in large bold script, with "greatest" underlined three times and "world" underlined once, an enthusiasm I didn't recognize or remember. Had the years between the photo and that evening at Jeff's worn down my affection? Or had the need to protect myself from the pain of his loss closed off what appeared to be a robust and loving relationship? Or was it just a young teenager's way of communicating with a distant father, vying for attention? I don't know, but it was important to my father to carry our pictures close, a gesture of sincere regard and love.

Behind the photos lay a resume of his busy life. He was a member of Rotary, the Plainview Country Club, the Texas Tech Red Raider Club, the International Flying Farmers. His hunting, driver's and commercial pilot's licenses were current to November 1966, as was his qualification as a flight instructor. Business cards from produce shippers as far away as California reflected the growing reach of Walker Brothers Produce. He carried an "A Rh positive" blood-type card and he even had proof of a smallpox vaccination, required to cross the US-Mexico border and possibly for the trip we had taken to Monterrey the year before. Dad had much to balance.

The wallet could have told a different story. It could have been devoid of family, without club memberships or licenses. Not all men carry family pictures on them. For example, my purse was stolen in Mexico once and my husband and I found ourselves at the US consulate trying to convince officials there that I was who I said I was in order to get a temporary entry visa back into the US. The officer asked Ed if he had a picture of me in his wallet. Embarrassingly, he didn't.

Dad's wallet reflected his full life with his commitment to his family, his community and his work. My wallet would have been just as full as my father's at age forty-nine—a time filled with children, husband, work, travel and community. We shared those commitments, a lesson I thought came from my mother but now realize also came from observing Dad.

SIXTEEN

Final Flight over
the Himalayas

T HE FINAL IMAGINED letter from my father is an amalgam of information from the Mont Jennings interview, from interviews with
Hump pilots and from my World War II research.

* * *

Misamari, India & Kunming, China
August 1945

Dear Mom and Dad,

I'm sorry I haven't written you much since I've been in India,
and you might not receive this letter before I get back to the States.
But I wanted to write you about how it has felt to fly the missions
from Misamari to Kunming and about my last day flying over the
Hump. I don't want to forget this experience, and today's flight was
really special.

This morning, as he always did when I fly, the CQ (Charge of
Quarters) shook me awake from under my mosquito netting with a
"You're wanted for flight, Lieutenant." It was still dark with just a
hint of light coming over the mountains. I woke up quickly, excited
and apprehensive at the same time. It was hard to believe that today

would be my last flight over the Hump—the dreaded last assignment that all pilots hope not to jinx after the hundreds of flights already taken successfully. When I first faced the Himalayas nine months ago, after hearing stories of the infamous weather, overloaded planes and constant instrument flying, I was anxious to get started, but I also suppressed a layer of fear. Today I was not cocky, but more confident. Last flights, though, are notoriously anxiety-provoking—so close and yet so much could still go wrong.

Over the last months I've made 149 missions, racking up enough hours in the air to finally head home as the war ends. The pace has been a challenging one—fly one day, have the night and part of the next day off. Then fly the night and have half of the day and the night off and fly again the next morning. Since there was very little to do in Misamari and virtually every day was filled with rain, flying was a relief and contributed to the hours needed to return home. I've had a couple of R&Rs at the Karnani Estates in Calcutta, a fun officers' hotel with good whiskey. I had hoped to get to Darjeeling for some cool air in the hill stations but that didn't work out. Mostly, I've just flown.

One disappointment has been the lack of camaraderie amongst the pilots. We fly with someone different every day, and our bunkmates are constantly moving in and out as they complete or begin their missions. We don't get to know each other well enough to kid around about a girlfriend or joke about the living conditions or even compare stories about the hazards of flying. Our schedules have been so varied that we can't even eat dinner together. I like talking to a stranger as much as anyone—getting his story, looking for shared experiences—but I've missed making real pals who can laugh at the retelling of stories about long hours, cold cockpits, the terror of downwind drafts. Just this morning I was thinking that finding a friend from home who is also flying the Hump would be most welcome, but it had never happened.

Despite the hazards of flight and the need to wear uncomfortable oxygen masks, I have enjoyed my time in the cockpit. On the rare beautiful day, our plane would climb to twenty thousand feet, sail smoothly over waves of snow-covered mountains and land just outside Kunming, an ancient trade town on the Guizhou Plateau in southwestern China. We use radio beacons placed along our route to track our correct location. When the Japanese were active, they would occasionally slyly take or move the markers to confuse our navigators, who keep us informed of our progress. Fortunately, the Japanese have now been gone for a few months.

Gasoline isn't the only cargo we've been carrying. One game played by pilots in the air or at mess is to talk about who has had the strangest loads. Mine have been pretty dull, but some guys have ferried livestock, Chinese soldiers who tried to jump out for fear of flying, and even a grand piano for Madame Chiang Kai-Shek. The most exciting had to have been crates of gold and a maharishi from Burma, who was probably fleeing the war chaos. Apparently, those crates weighed much more than the standard gasoline barrel.

In Kunming, the only airport linking China to the outside world at the onset of the war, the barrels of gasoline are unloaded by a whole swarm of coolies, Chinese men and women dressed in pants, button-down jackets, sandals and bibbed hats. Often in landing, I see other Chinese workers using their baskets to carry rocks to maintain the runway.

Because of the food in Kunming, we all liked our time there. It was simple: They always had fresh eggs and vegetables, a welcome reprieve from our rations of powered eggs, powdered milk and Spam. And we got some time to catch a nap, especially if we'd been flying through the night. Only once did a plane of mine need some repair before we could return. As a result, I got a chance to go into downtown Kunming for some of their famous sweet and sour pork. The town is active these days, serving as a refugee center for the many Chinese who have fled from the Japanese. While I was in downtown Kunming, I bought a bong, the Chinese water pipe, as a souvenir, but I avoided the Chinese cigarettes. They're cheap but potent, scorching the lungs on the inhale. The army has provided us with enough American cigarettes.

This morning the jeep dropped me off at my C-47. Despite the greater numbers of C-46s available, I'm still a little partial to the C-47 because of its reliability. I was loaded with the usual map case, parachute and a 45-caliber pistol loaded with three bullets, to kill animals for food or to shoot at charging elephants if I had to jump into the jungle below. A trench knife in my shoulder holster serves two purposes: to increase my odds of survival in the jungle and to cut loose from the parachute if I were to get entangled in a tree upon landing. I've heard of many crew members who have survived bailouts because of the survival paraphernalia provided in the kit. I've been fortunate that I have never needed any of these items.

Once out of the jeep, I followed my usual routine. I inspected the plane's exterior, looking for oil or gas leaks and damage, especially from the crushed rock runway in Kunming. Inside, I surveyed the cargo to be sure the weight was distributed evenly.

Now here's the great surprise: When I climbed into the cockpit, I met up with Mont Jennings, a pilot from Lubbock. Can you believe that we live only 45 miles apart in Texas and ended up in the same plane in India during the war? There was an instant rapport. We talked of the Panhandle, of Texas Tech, of farming, of High Plains storms. Although we compared acquaintances, we couldn't find any direct connections, only our shared location.

Behind us was our crew chief and flight engineer. In the two hours since its arrival from China, our plane had been loaded with the usual barrels of gasoline. That cargo was always heavy, dangerous and distinctive-smelling, and I won't miss the tinderbox-feel I always have when flying with it behind me. My radio operator was listening to a pilot up in the air giving the Kunming weather report, already four hours old. Lots can change in those hours, but I felt lucky. The weather was good there too, and maybe it would hold. As always, I consulted with the last flight crew for any advice, followed the step-by-step checklist, looked at the flight plan one last time and made a final check of the oxygen system, just to be sure it was working. It was essential to my survival.

I was so relieved that the day stayed clear. You just can't imagine the storms here, Dad. Sudden thunderstorms cause violent updrafts and downdrafts, and ice can form on the wings. We either have to use wipers to prevent a heavy buildup or drop to a warmer altitude for the ice to melt. Icing can also slow the plane down. Today, I wasn't going to have to deal with any of that. As we crossed the homing beacon at the Myitkyina base, our needle swung round confirming the location, and I turned the plane left to 103 degrees for the 119-mile leg to Paoshan. All was going smoothly.

We tried to pick up Tokyo Rose on the radio. You've probably heard about her. She's the Japanese American who tries to scare American and British soldiers with propaganda stories of Japanese successes. I always chuckled at her attempts, but I did enjoy the current American music she played. Today, we couldn't rouse anything on the radio. But I didn't care since this was my last flight.

I was the pilot on the way in, enjoying a last view of Mount Tali with its monastery on top. Our approach into Kunming was over the large Lake Tien Ch'ih, or Dian Chi, always a challenge at the end of a three-and-a-half hour flight when the crew is tired. Traffic around Kunming was stacked up, requiring each plane to let down five hundred feet at a time. Once on the ground, another jeep led us to the hangers, past a sign on the control tower that read "You Made It Again", my 150th trip.

From there, Jennings and I knew where to head: the mess hall, where we hoped bacon or even fried chicken might be available today. It was a good meal but nothing like your cooking, Mom. I can't wait to get back to your kitchen!

We got a few hours of sleep before returning. Jennings did the flying on the way back, happily an uneventful flight since the weather cooperated. I had my last view of the Himalayas, knowing I won't be back anytime soon and recognizing that I've had an experience that will be hard to describe back home.

So here I am, in my bache for the last time. I've had the two shots of South African combat whiskey that we're allowed at the end of every mission. Jennings and I drank ours together. After today I'll probably get sent to Calcutta for the ship home. Within the month, I should be stateside and can make my way home. I've often wondered if the people back in the USA even know about our effort over here. I guess I'll find out soon enough.

I'll call as soon as I can. I'm ready to start life again, find a wife(!), maybe farm. Who knows how it will play out. But one thing I'm sure of. Now that I've conquered the highest mountain range in the world, I will always fly.

I'll be seeing you very soon.

Love,

Charlie

My father at Kunming Airport, 1945. Words on the side of the building *(left)*: YOU MADE IT AGAIN—GOOD WORK!"

SEVENTEEN

Flying with Dad

It is late May 1966. My mother likes to travel as soon as school is out, trying to stay ahead of the crowd. She has a high school friend living in Seattle, and we're paying a first time visit to her. Dad's newest plane is a Bonanza six-seater, big enough for the family to fly together. We approach the plane, tuck our luggage in the small storage area in the back and climb in. The seats are worn, a bit musty, infused with the smell of fuel. Low seats and elevated windows make viewing difficult below but glorious to see above. As always, Dad, the seasoned World War II pilot, sits confidently in the pilot's seat.

Hours later, after a stop in Grand Junction, Colorado, we approach Boise Idaho, then just a town with a small airport, nestled in a valley. Landing is routine, and the family slowly unwinds out of the plane looking for bathrooms. After the plane is refueled, we reenter the plane in order—the three younger brothers in the back two seats, my older brother and me in the middle row, and our parents in the front seats. Dad moves the plane toward the end of the short runway. I notice for the first time that the landing strip ends just as the steep mountain begins, leaving little room for error.

Dad doesn't appear worried. He revs up the motor, pushing the propeller's rpm higher, and the plane shakes as he finally releases the brake. The plane slowly advances, gradually gaining speed. The mountain looms closer. My mother's eyes dart from Dad to the mountain and back, making the rest of us quietly anxious. Dad holds the plane down until the last second, pulling up as the runway disappears, immediately banking sharply to the left to avoid the trees. We quickly gain altitude, and soon town and airport lie far below.

* * *

THIS WAS THE only time I was ever nervous flying with Dad. I had flown with him for years—short jaunts in his small Piper and now longer trips. After returning from World War II, he always had his own plane and would occasionally take a child or two up on a Sunday afternoon. A trip to nearby Lubbock meant a stop for a Coke from the vending machine at the private section of the terminal. He loved to push the plane into a stall and make us squeal as the plane seemed to stop flying. As we got older, he would turn the wheel over and instruct us to keep the plane level with the horizon. That wasn't easy when you were too short to see the horizon, but it was still thrilling to think you had control of the plane.

With the larger Bonanza, we now ventured to Dallas on family outings. There was often an airport car we could use, available to visiting pilots. I always liked the terminal for private planes. It was set apart from the commercial one for the airlines. Dad would park the plane next to other private ones on the open space in front of the terminal, leaving room for each to pull out. After years of flying commercial airlines since my father's death, I now recognize the freedom we had of simply walking from the plane on the tarmac into the terminal, where large windows provided easy viewing of the runways. Rows of seats were available for waiting, and cool maps on the walls provided coordinates that only pilots would readily understand. The terminal was rarely crowded. World War II veteran pilots dominated the scene, and it was unusual for a family our size to pull in.

Mom and Dad occasionally took a trip with another couple or two. One story had them in Denver, needing to get back home but with a storm approaching. Mom recounted the nervousness of everyone except my father. He decided they could make it by flying toward a single hole in the dark clouds. After takeoff the group resolved to talk to take their minds off the anxiety of escaping the nearby turbulent weather. Yet after agreeing to do that, not another word was spoken until the plane broke into sunshine ahead of the front. Dad never showed any concern.

As flying was an early part of our lives growing up, I didn't associate it with anything special. That was Dad's thing. With so many World War II veterans returning home, there were many pilots, even in our small town, and planes were readily available thanks to the large production during the war. The Plainview airport had one commercial service, Trans-Texas Airways (later Texas International Airlines and then Continental Airlines), that landed twice a day. Plane ownership wasn't something I tried to drop into a conversation, even though I was proud of having one and a father who could fly it. A new acquaintance in town once commented that she was telling her cousins about Plainview and our friendship and that we had a plane. She had never known anyone with a plane, and I had never thought of our ownership in that way, as something exclusive.

When I visited with cousins and some close friends, the plane was a big part of their memory of Dad and our family. He was generous in offering them rides and never required a parent's consent. One of my older brother's friends rode for the first time with Dad and Mack to return from a skiing trip. He confessed that the ride hooked him, and he became a professional pilot.

At my fiftieth high school reunion, classmate Robert Carter, whose family was close to ours, astonished me with his memory of Dad. In the early 1950s, my family of seven was living in a small two-bedroom rock house northwest of Plainview, with a farm in back that Dad leased. Robert's family owned land across the highway and they would often visit. Robert remembered being in the backyard with all the kids when my father flew over in his plane and landed on one of the dirt roads that divided the tracts of farmland behind the house. Dad jumped out of the plane like he was getting out of his pickup as Robert described it, acknowledged the children in the yard with a big hello and disappeared into the house to have lunch with Mom. Later, he emerged, waved to the children again, climbed back into the plane and took off. It was an *Out of Africa* moment, with Dad instead of Robert Redford flying the plane. He had probably just made a crop-dusting run and was close to the house, rather than flying over herds of elephants and hippos in Africa. But I loved the image—the World War II pilot cockiness, knowing the conditions were right to land on a dirt road, wanting to join his wife for lunch.

Despite not recalling Robert's story, I kept thinking about it, trying to coax up a memory. Since memories can be malleable, I feared I might adopt Robert's story as mine, rather than truly remembering it. But after hearing his story, my cousin Carolyn said, "I do remember a plane being

My mother (*center*) with friends getting into a plane that my father will pilot.

parked at your farm home." And suddenly, it was there: I knew exactly where the plane had parked: behind the detached garage, at the edge of the farm—a memory recovered.

This journey has been filled with such recoveries, jarred by a photo, a friend's story, a quiet moment of reflection—each building a fuller picture of my father, something I had thought no longer possible. I now appreciate and even enjoy my father more than I did as a young daughter, each memory making me feel closer to the man who kept his distance when alive.

It was years after my father's early death before I thought seriously about Dad's calmness and confidence in flying. It took the journey to retrace his World War II footsteps before I understood the depth of his flying life in the war and afterward. Only in retrospect did I realize why Dad never broke stride in taking off from that airport in Idaho. Those mountains were nothing compared to the Himalayas. The runway was probably longer than the one he'd had in India, and the cargo lighter. Pushing ahead of a Colorado storm was simple compared to the down and updrafts he had encountered when a storm from the Gobi Desert collided with the cold air above the peaks of the Himalayas. Air pockets over the Arizona desert could easily be anticipated. Radio confirmation of his location was available when he flew with us, rather than the dead reckoning sometimes required during the war. This was easy for him. He had seen much worse.

FAMILY MEMORIES

EIGHTEEN

Mom Finds Her Way

As with everything I am trying to find out about my father, I don't try to explore Mom's relationship with Dad until much too late. After my discovery of the Mont Jennings tape and the decision to travel to India and China, I want to ask Mom what she still remembers about Dad. She is eighty-seven and has dementia, but I hope to coax some memories from her.

I sit beside her in her living room and we chat about her past. I ask for recollections of Dad—what she loved about him, why she married him, what she has missed the most. Her memory loss does not stop her from describing her mean stepmother and the many chores she made Mom do. It does not prevent a recollection of hard times during the Depression. Mom is quick to complain about those parts of her past. But in answer to my questions about Dad, she just smiles and says, "He was nice to me."

* * *

MY MOTHER AND I never had a serious conversation about my father or his death. She died soon after my attempt above. With sadness and frustration with myself, I had to close the door to what should have been my best source. In the past, we had nibbled around the edges of candor and openness with an occasional innocuous question from me such as "Did Dad like to read?" or an observation from Mom at a child's wedding, as in "Charlie would have loved this." Even those tidbits were rare, possibly because of Mom's past coping methods when a tragedy hit.

My mother was a survivor. After losing both parents before she was nineteen and her husband when she was forty-five, she had every reason to be depressed and bitter, but she wasn't. During her childhood, she found friends' mothers who nurtured her. A favorite aunt and uncle took her in after her father's death. An adored grandmother paid for her college. High school friends walked with her every step. Mom brought an optimistic resilience to life that carried her through each crisis. That may be the reason why we never explored our feelings about Dad's death and that I only caught occasional comments about their relationship. She needed to move on as she had done all her life, resisting pensive or painful thoughts.

After Dad's death, though, Mom was visibly sad. Missing from her usual welcoming eyes was the trademark brightness. The ready smile was slower and diminished. She seemed absent from dinner table conversation and I missed her participation. No one sat in my father's place at the head of the table for a long while, with Mack eventually replacing Dad. At New Year's that first year, Mom refused to eat any black-eyed peas, a traditional Southern dish for good luck. She said, "It didn't do me any good last year." It was years before Mom could give away Dad's clothes.

I knew Mom was in pain. The first Christmas without him was particularly hard. It was the only Christmas I can remember when Mom didn't overdo the holiday. She had always loved the entire season, decorating every nook of our big house, often hosting parties, preparing baked goods for friends and neighbors, and buying all five of us a big present from Santa Claus, two presents for under the tree and small gifts for the stockings. But Christmas 1966 was subdued. The only hint of humor came with the purchase of the Christmas tree, something Dad had always done. In our inexperience, we selected a malformed tree with far fewer branches on one side than on the other. Gary tried to even it out by cutting off a lower branch from one side, drilling a hole in the bare side and sticking in the branch. The natural branches arched slightly upward. The extra branch stuck straight out, perpendicular to the trunk. One look at the finished product and we all laughed out loud at the pitiful tree. Then we laughed some more, with tears running down our faces. We

Our first Christmas tree without my father.

laughed every time we looked at the tree. Mom said it felt good to laugh, a first since Dad's death.

I didn't know what to say to her after Dad died, and she didn't talk to us. Since my parents' relationship appeared loving, her failure to talk much about Dad was surprising. Maybe she was just trying to protect us by not bringing up the sad subject of his death. Maybe that was her now-familiar mode of dealing with tragedy: bearing it without complaining, not wanting to bring down her friends and family with tears. Maybe she opened up with her friends but not with her children. Or maybe it was the norm for the times. Many families had lost loved ones during the war and just moved on. That would have been Mom's model. It became mine too, and it served me well as I built a new life without the pain of reflecting on what had been lost. Only on this journey have I understood that the pain was always there, masked by everyday life.

Later, Mom would say it was her children who saved her. That's because she didn't have the luxury of withdrawing from life, not even for a short time. Mack was seventeen and graduating, I was sixteen and needed to visit and soon apply to colleges, the younger brothers were in band, sports and Boy Scouts and played baseball. Planning meals, attending band concerts, signing the younger boys up for little league baseball, ordering a graduation robe for Mack, helping with the Junior-Senior Prom...all these were diversions that kept memories of Dad at a distance. Life needed her attention, and somehow, she found the fortitude to keep going. It couldn't have been easy.

At the beginning of her single life, my mother had to settle Dad's estate. Decisions had to be made about the assets, whether to sell Dad's businesses and the terms of any possible sale...what to do with his plane, (would any of the kids want to fly?); should the farm be sold? (would any of the boys want to farm?). A conflict with Dad's life insurance company over the cause of his death required the threat of a lawsuit and resulted in a delay in receiving the proceeds. Mom never consulted the children about those problems or decisions, relying instead on a trusted family attorney. It must have been disorienting for her. Single mothers were rare in my childhood, leaving her without a role model. Since men dominated the business and professional worlds, she had to learn to navigate those worlds without a man. She also had to adjust to a more isolated social life.

Two years after Dad died, I was in college at Trinity University in San Antonio, experiencing loneliness for the first time. The transition to college life had been more difficult than I had expected, with a college roommate who was heavily into drugs and in a rule-laden school that offered few activities. When I came back to school from a weekend in Austin in the fall, I found a sign posted on the door by my roommate to enter quietly. She had tripped on acid and needed to sleep it off. Coming from a small town, I wasn't yet that rebellious and didn't know how to maneuver in this new world, with its freedom to push the limits.

Long-distance calls cost by the minute back then, making phone conversations short. Mom and I talked only briefly and only on Sundays, with quick inquiries about what each had been doing. Her stories of home and my brothers were meant to fill the time with light conversation, but they only reminded me of the secure life I had left behind. I hesitated to share my loneliness because I didn't want to worry her. The saddest moment of the week was when I hung up the phone from those weekly calls.

We did write letters, though. After the second anniversary of Dad's death, I opened a letter from Mom, expecting the usual friendly, encouraging message. Instead, it angrily accused me of not having recognized the date in any way and added that I had been selfish for not thinking about her. This was out of character for her. I had never experienced such an outburst from her, and it hurt. I didn't think until much later that she was just missing Dad, but the letter was still shocking and painful. I didn't want to minimize Mom's changed circumstances, but I was having my own problems. I wrote back, apologizing for failing to acknowledge the date. But I also told her that it had been hard for me in school, having to answer questions about my father when asked by the many new people I was meeting. I told her she was lucky to be in Plainview, where everyone knew of Dad's death and where she didn't have to constantly explain how and when it had happened. Mom had never thought about my situation and was apologetic. We never mentioned it again.

Mom missed having a man around. As independent as she was, she still felt that men and women played different parts, a division of labor that I always chafed at but which was more common in her generation. Some things she particularly hated to do. Paying for a meal, for example, always caused her to panic. Figuring the tip was the problem. It wasn't the ten percent. She could do that. But she didn't want to appear cheap. Soon after Dad's death, a waiter complained to her about his tip and she was traumatized by the incident for the rest of her life, always wishing that Dad that was there to do that "man's" job.

My husband and I turned forty-nine in the same year, and I reflected often on my parents during those twelve months. That was the age my father died. We had a sister-in-law who had died a year earlier at that same age and another dear friend who did too. How devastating it would have been to lose my husband at that age, at a time when children were testing their parents and seismic changes were at hand with college approaching. It was the sixties and seventies after Dad died, and my brothers and I were not perfect. Mom had to maneuver those turbulent years alone. And even though I had a good career as an attorney, my husband was at his peak earning capacity at forty-nine, and the financial loss would have equaled that of my mother's. As a pediatrician, my husband was as absent as was my father, but he was still available in the evenings to talk and process problems and to give love and support. I thought of all that I would miss about Ed—his involvement with the children, his sense of humor, his love of music and dancing, his openness to travel and his cheerful greeting that came with a kiss when he got home in the evening. I would be without physical and emotional intimacy, long walks and the needed "I love you" at the end of a day. My mother lost all that, and I ached for her loss.

By putting all these memories together, I am comforted by the positive relationship that I now see existed between my parents and by the rich times they enjoyed together. Despite the brevity of their marriage, it was filled with action, each spouse giving the other space to do what needed to be done—Dad at work and Mom at home. This made my mother's inability to remember even a single story about Dad so surprising, even at her advanced age. What she remembered, though, was the way he made her feel. No personal stories of falling in love. No excitement of marriage or life together. Just a feeling. Even though I couldn't coax any more information from her, I understood why Mom remembered only that part. She had to overcome many tragedies in her life, working through the attendant insecurities caused by those upheavals. She was always sensitive to how people treated her. And Dad treated her well. That part she remembered.

Family photo taken six years after my father's death. *Front row, left to right:* My brothers Gary, Morey, and Mack. *Second Row:* Me, my mother, Mildred Walker, and my brother Jeff.

NINETEEN

Fifty Years After My Father's Death: November 8, 2016

Before I started this journey, I couldn't have recalled the exact date of my father's death. I write that with appropriate embarrassment. Too much time had passed with too many intervening wedding dates and children's birthdates.

It is now three weeks prior to our departure for India and I finally realize that this year, 2016, is fifty years after Dad's death, an amazing enough coincidence. But then I compare our tickets with his death certificate and realize that we are leaving for India exactly a day after that fiftieth anniversary. Is that providential? Serendipity? I suppose that depends on your belief system. I just know that my brothers and I need to acknowledge the date, that we need to finally communicate about Dad. It is time to try, and I hope my brothers will agree.

* * *

I LOVE MY brothers. They are great company and share some common qualities: They are all hard-working, smart, calm, analytical in a good way, organized, and good dads and husbands. Mack and Morey became civil engineers. Both used Dad's entrepreneurial skills with Mack becoming highly successful in the consulting engineering field and Morey to eventually own his own business. Gary's shy nature kept him a company man, valued for his ability to learn and develop software for banks. Jeff's outgoing personality landed him in sales, where he continued the family's agricultural tradition by dealing in boatloads of fruit and vegetables from foreign countries. My cousin Barbara has described Jeff's personality as being the most like our father's, giving me a new way of looking at my youngest brother, discovering that his easy-going nature has a genetic component.

Two brothers followed Dad's interest in flying. Gary got his license soon after high school but didn't maintain it for long. Morey waited until his fifties before learning to fly and even built his own plane with a friend.

Mack wanted to carry on the family farming tradition and did try for a year. But without a father to help with the initial costs and to guide him, he realized that engineering was a more reliable career.

My brothers and I spread across the country—California, New Mexico and two spots in Texas. Mom spent weeks of her time each year visiting us individually, and we tried to unite at least once every year or two. When we gathered as adults, our spouses and children would be in tow. The stories then would be about funny things our kids did, frustrations with work, politics, family vacations and easy banter about golf scores. Serious topics like religion, emotions, depression or finances were never discussed. And that included talk about Dad. We never talked about him, just as he never talked about his past. We were following his unfortunate model of silence.

My husband has always said that every individual contends with death differently. When I would tell friends or acquaintances that my brothers and I didn't talk about our father or his death, I got looks—expressions of surprise, questioning, arched eyebrows, a rare nod of understanding. And then there were the comments like "really?" and the inevitable, "Why not?" I've never found a good answer to that last question, although much has been written about grief. I have encountered this silence and failure to talk in works of fiction, but those stories usually involve traumatic events involving the deceased parent. Since Dad didn't leave us emotionally scarred by his treatment of us, none of us felt a later need for counseling. His sudden departure just left a void that was masked by our activities. Truthfully, because of Dad's frequent absences, our daily routine didn't change much.

We weren't the only family who failed to talk of a deceased parent. Pat, my best friend in high school, lost her father at a much earlier age and she confirmed that nothing was said about her dad after the funeral. It just went dark, like the song in *The Book of Mormon* that suggests you "turn it off" for any sad feelings you have. I never asked Pat about him and she never offered to share the story. Another friend's father deserted the family, while another's dad divorced his mother and disappeared. Those stories weren't pursued either. Maybe this resilience was a holdover from pioneer days in the Texas Panhandle when life simply had to move on. Maybe it was the just the philosophy of the time—out of sight, out of mind.

Mack left for college nine months after Dad's death. I departed a year after that. Within five more years, all of us had left Plainview for our education, leaving behind the many who had known Dad and their stories about him.

In the middle of this journey to rediscover my father, I contacted my brothers about a description of Dad that I had received from his extended family. Aunt Winnie had described Dad as the most outgoing, the favorite brother who loved to tease all the younger sisters. I wrote cousins about their memories, and they responded with how much they loved Uncle Charlie. He was their favorite uncle. He was so much fun. Several of them used that same word. Fun. The word stunned me. I had never thought of my father as fun. I remember staring at that word. How could I not remember my father as fun? I had to talk to my brothers about it. I called each one and asked, "Do you remember Dad as being fun?" None could. None of us would ever have used that adjective in describing our father. Yet our cousins did.

It was then, after hanging up with my last brother, after having caught only glimpses of the man beneath the "Dad veneer," of aching to know more about him and his war experiences, after the frustration of dead ends of research, after reading too many obituaries of family friends and their now-lost memories of Dad, that I cried. At age sixty-six, I cried with an intensity I hadn't thought possible. How could I not have known he was fun? How did we miss that? Was he so busy providing for all of us and being the occasional disciplinarian that he couldn't relax around the family? And why did he not talk to us about his youth or war days? The regrets of those fifty years piled up and I cried, experiencing an unexpected nadir in my otherwise uplifting search.

A recent favorite movie of mine is *Coco*, an animated film in which a young boy ventures into the magical world of the dead in search of his grandfather, who had died many years before. The tradition only allows those of the dead who are still remembered in the real world by others to come back to mingle with the living on the Day of the Dead holiday. After meeting his grandfather among the dead, the little boy returns to encourage his grandmother to remember her husband so that he can come see her on the Day of the Dead. On the fiftieth anniversary of our father's death, I felt that my brothers and I needed to do the same—to think intensely about Dad, to pull any details we could remember to the surface. We needed to let Dad visit us for a while.

I wrote each brother, asking him to delve deep into his memories of our father and to send them in an email to the rest of us on that anniversary, on November 8, 2016. Mack was seventeen when Dad died, and I assumed that he would remember the most. Jeff was only eleven, and I figured that he would have the hardest time remembering.

I didn't hear anything back about this request. I didn't know if they planned to write or not. That wasn't unusual. As fond of my brothers as I am, they have this one small, common flaw: a lack of communication. Unacknowledged emails are regular experiences. They mean to but often don't. Follow-up calls or emails are needed. For this request, I would have to wait and see, wondering whether their stories could lead me down a rabbit hole of experiences.

TWENTY

Scarce Memories

ON THE MORNING of November 8, I waited. I wasn't going to write first, although I had already composed an essay of my recollections. I had been immersed in this project for some time, and had re-awakened many memories in the process.

Gary's Memories

About 10:00 a.m., a short email arrived from Gary. He sent a list:

- *Running through the parking lot with him after a high school football game.*
- *Waiting in a pickup while he yelled and cussed at some people that were stealing some potatoes from the farm.*
- *Teaching me how to fill a tractor with propane gas and then teaching me how to drive it.*
- *I remember him taking us kids to the shed, and we had the run of the place.*
- *The bright spotlight when he filmed us with the 8mm movie camera.*

I stared a long time at the list. Two were familiar—the run of the shed and the spotlight on the 8mm movie camera—but I had forgotten them. They made me smile. We always had to wait on Christmas mornings to see our presents from Santa Claus while Dad got the newest movie camera ready for our entrance. The lights were incredibly bright.

The other memories were personal to Gary. It was such a small list, indicative of time passed and the absence of our father through much of our childhood. But they brought out Dad's temper and determination to protect his crops, a characteristic that I had learned from my cousin's story of Dad wanting to fight his brother over which crops to plant. It's no surprise that Gary would remember our father's willingness to teach his son about a tractor and propane, and that he would attend football games with the family. Retained memories often center around how we are treated, as Gary's did.

Thanks to Gary's memory of the bright movie spotlight, Dad became a 1940s and '50s techie guy in my eyes, starting with his fascination with airplanes and his early use of still and movie cameras. He was the only dad I knew who had a two-way radio in his car; he used it to talk to the produce shed when needed. It must have reminded him of talking in his plane to the control tower during World War II, with the alternating speaking and having to say "over" when you finished talking so that the other side could reply. I loved being in the car when the call came in from the shed, usually from Mario Trevino, the manager, his voice crackling through the air, trying to find Dad for Mom. If Dad were alive today, I feel certain he would have the latest iPhone.

While I would never characterize myself as a techie, I do love trying new things, exploring new places, meeting new people, hearing new ideas. I long thought that Mom's side of family had passed that gene down, but it appears Dad played some part in this characteristic.

Jeff's Memories

Jeff's email came in next, also as a list:

Moments, Pieces…
- *Clam-digging on a trip to Seattle with him. Remember getting up real early to do it. Remember it was cold digging in the sand for them AND Mack complaining that it was way too early for him (Sorry Mack!).*
- *Remember flying across the desert of Arizona on our trip to Calif. Especially the hot air pockets.*
- *Driving fast in the Fury on dirt roads to farm.*
- *Free peanuts at the shed. Assume it was a gift to him from suppliers, maybe.*

• Coors when he did drink, I believe.
• I still have the 8mm projector in my garage.
• The one action I really remember the most was the night he had the stroke.
I was standing in the doorway between the kitchen and the big living room.
He was heading out the door to go back to shed, turned and waved goodbye
to me. It stands out 'cause of what happened later that night.

None of us will forget that flight across the Arizona desert. My father tried to prepare us, knowing that the flight through the hot air pockets would be rough, insisting that the family take Dramamine. We all did except Mack, who wanted to be like Dad and tough it out. Of course, none of us realized that Dad was so experienced, having flown in much worse weather and through much harsher air pockets during the war. And, Dad was the pilot and couldn't take any medication that would make him sleepy. Dramamine did the trick for the rest of the family as we were pushed up and down by the hot air pockets in the stuffy plane cabin. Mack was not so fortunate.

Jeff's memories nudged mine. I had to be reminded of driving fast with Dad in his Plymouth Fury across farm roads and of peanuts at the shed. It was amusing to have those memories drift back in from a closed part of my mind. Even those small memories gave a more accurate portrayal of Dad—the fun-loving part that we had all forgotten or failed to observe or appreciate, whether he was driving fast or drinking a Coors when relaxing.

It was the final memory that brought tears—so poignant, so personal, so long silently held. Jeff had the last interaction with Dad, even though he was the youngest. None of us would get to talk to our father again. We would only see him once more, on a respirator in a hospital. Jeff's was the memory I most want to remember: the father headed back to work after dinner, putting in long hours to support his family, turning to wave goodbye to his youngest child.

Morey's Memories

Morey's memories came next. Mo was always slow to respond, and I was afraid we wouldn't hear from him. His were also personal:

I remember some experiences with Dad…
• I do remember him letting me sit on his lap to fly the plane. He kept

*saying to keep the plane level by looking at the horizon but I never could
see over the panel to find the horizon.*
*• Once, the family was on a trip and Dad and I had to share a bed. He
was snoring like crazy so I hit him in the mouth with the back of my
hand. He didn't like that too much but didn't say anything until the
next morning.*
*• He let the kids ride in the cotton trailers to the compress and pulled the
kids in sleds behind the green Plymouth during snowstorms. I don't think
either was very safe, but somehow we lived through childhood.*
*• I once let go a series of farts that Dad thought was funny. He said they
sounded like a machine gun. I was pretty proud of myself.*
*• One time, Mom and Dad went to Mexico and he brought me back a
pair of silver cufflinks. I am not sure what a ten-year-old kid was going
to do with silver cufflinks but they are now my most prized item. It is
the only thing I remember that Dad gave me.*

As with Gary and Jeff, Morey's memories were small in number. I
focused on the silver cufflinks. Cufflinks are in rare use these days but
weren't then. They were worn with tuxedos and some nicer shirts. Dad
was always a sharp dresser and I could envision him looking to buy something for Morey and thinking ahead to a future use for a graduation or
wedding. The real miracle was that Morey kept up with the cufflinks for
fifty years through college and many moves. They were his only direct
connection to Dad, making them prized.

Consistent through Morey's memories was Dad's easygoing streak—
letting us ride in the cotton trailers, handing over the steering wheel of
our plane and pulling us behind a car on a snow sled. I started noting a
pattern of actions over words: Even if none of us could quote Dad, we remembered how we felt when he reached out to us.

Morey's email began a series of responses from the rest of us. Jeff thought
that we had been pulled on a truck's inner tube across a field of snow.
Morey observed that he didn't miss those burr haircuts that Dad gave
every few weeks. They hurt and he strangled them with towels. That jarred
Jeff's memory of the blue high-chair where they had to sit for the haircuts.
Gary remembered rabbit hunting in the Plymouth Fury. I was savoring
the exchange, the thawing of memories, the lightening up of my image of

Dad, each story like a creek spilling into a larger river-view of our father. We were late sharing, but there were still stories to tell.

Mack's Memories

"Family, well I'm a little tardy in putting together my recollections of Dad but here goes…

"Very patient and understanding. One of my first tractor-driving adventures was to run a mower-type blade over a new field of carrots. The purpose of the mowing was to cut the weeds that were popping up above the carrots. Dad set the height and left me to finish the job. Well, he came back in a few hours and unknown to me the mower had lowered (due to a leaky hydraulic tubing), and I had not only cut the weeds but the carrot tops. So it looked like a mowed yard. I thought I had ruined the whole crop. Dad just looked at it, acknowledged the problem and went about his business. Luckily, the carrots recovered and we were able to harvest the crop later.

"The second episode was when I overturned the Anglia during my trip home for lunch. As usual, I tried to race and as I did later with the cousins, I overturned the car into a ditch. Dad happened to be coming home for lunch and found me and the car. He just shook his head and pulled me out of the ditch."

The last brother to respond was Mack. He and his wife, Jan, were already traveling in India on the anniversary of Dad's death and all he wrote was a promise to share his experiences when he returned, which he did. I have used some of his memories in other parts of the book.

As the oldest, Mack's birth order was evident in the large number of memories he had of Dad. In engineer fashion, he had the paragraphs numbered and identified by eight subjects, such as "businessman," "recreation" and "sense of humor." The stories were mostly new to me, confirming our lack of communication over the years, our failure to reminisce. After the funeral, we dimmed the lights over his memory, waiting fifty years to push the rheostat back up.

Mack worked on our farm and in the shed during middle and high school and had a closer connection to Dad. I read and reread his memories and was envious. He had so many—probably the difference between him being the oldest boy and me the only girl. While I was ironing handker-chiefs and shirts at home in the summer, Mack was up early eating bacon and eggs before heading to the fields with Dad. They didn't talk much but they did work together. Mom taught me to sew and Dad instructed Mack on how to start an irrigation pipe and drive a tractor. I got to watch Mom's soap operas while Mack was getting a farmer's tan. Even then, it didn't seem quite fair, but I would never have thought of asking Dad if I could come along and he only knew of the more traditional male-female roles. On the other hand, he never voiced any suggestion that I was to do what girls usually did which, in retrospect, left me open to find my own independent way as an adult without guilt, a previously unrealized and unacknowledged gift.

I loved the stories of Dad's calm response to Mack's teenage mishaps. After getting to know my father better through this journey, I realize that he must have been laughing on the inside when he saw the carrots and the overturned car. I can imagine him shaking his head, then tending to the situation. They were funny stories he would tell my mother or his friends when we weren't around. And his unperturbed response mirrors the way his children respond in an emergency. We share the ability to quickly an-alyze the real problem and are slow to allot blame or exhibit anger. I had never put that together before.

Many of Mack's stories helped me remember Dad as a more complete person. With so many things on his mind, he could appear absent-minded, like the time he forgot about Mack and left him at the shed when he went home for lunch. And there was no treating his children differently than he did his other employees at work. Mack worked at the ice company Dad had just bought and was set to earn a low rate of fifty cents an hour. The manager thought that inadequate, and to Mack's relief he upped the salary to seventy-five cents an hour.

One other story of Mack's stood out for me. It contributed to a growing list of fun memories of my father that I never expected:

> *"Sense of humor. Many summers Dad would hire some of our friends to help on the farm and the harvest. One summer Brian Fagan and Gary Covey were working on the potato harvester. Basically, they had to stand next to a conveyor belt and remove dirt clods from the belt.*

Well, one time they were working and for some reasons there were dirt clods coming from the air and pelting the harvester. They couldn't figure it out until they looked around and there was Dad lobbing clods at them and laughing the whole time."

Mack's email fit the emerging description of Dad that I had been accumulating: patient, hard-working, a good businessman, a sense of humor and, the most revealing and important, a man who was willing to take a risk and be different. His many businesses. Driving a Plymouth Fury—fast. Flying with his entire family in the same plane. Bringing home tequila from Mexico and learning how to dance the twist. This was not a shy, withdrawn man, even though he didn't talk a lot. His life was filled with new adventures and opportunities, and he took them.

Dad on vaction with my brothers. *Right to left*: Jeff, Morey and Gary.

TWENTY-ONE

My Memories

*"The recognition the town gave him in Rotary and on a bank board.
His early smoking, later ended, and his enjoyment of an occasional
beer…*

*"He attended a Girls' Friendly Society Father-Daughter banquet
with me. In the photo commemorating the event, I'm seated in a skirt
and white blouse with a GFS beanie on my head, my feet not touching
the ground. Dad is leaning back in his chair, dressed in a nice suit,
smiling more broadly than I think the event would have merited. All
the dads in the picture were smiling…*

*"Spring storms on the covered back porch with the family snuggling
under blankets watching the rain…*

*"He liked salt on his watermelon and on his tomatoes. He often
brought home fresh vegetables from the farm in the summer. I don't
remember him grilling outside. I have no idea what he did in the winter
when the fields lay fallow…*

*"The only fun thing I remember doing with him was in the
swimming pool: He would toss us in the air and into the water…"*

* * *

I WROTE THESE memories before receiving my brothers' recollections. The
greatest discovery from the exchange of emails with my brothers was
seeing a fun side of Dad emerge. He could have stayed inside in front of

With Dad at a Girls' Friendly Society banquet, 1960.

the TV after a snowstorm, but he didn't. He could have, out of caution, refused to fly his family in his plane or let us take the wheel. He could have turned down parties at his house or vacations to Mexico with Mom. And he could have driven the standard farm pickup instead of a Plymouth Sports Fury. He didn't have to be a fast-quipping Dad to be considered fun. His actions were proof enough.

For this fiftieth anniversary gathering of memories, I added some observational ones. Through my previous months of research and writing, Dad had started to come into focus as a standup guy, but it was superficial at first. Since I couldn't remember anything he said, I began watching him, putting myself in the picture of his actions, allowing my maturity to infer traits, to note what was missing, to see patterns in his life. Some of what I wrote that day is above and some I incorporated into my writing for this book. Just the exercise of challenging us all to share our memories on the fiftieth anniversary triggered many more.

After Mack sent his memories, the thread stopped. We didn't share any more experiences in writing. It was as though we were exhausted from the effort needed to reawaken all those long-repressed memories, limited though they were. We know from studies that traumatic events can cause memories to be buried. Dad's death was traumatic, more than I wanted to admit. Memories associated with emotions are more likely to surface easily, but in the case of my father's death, the emotion was too much. Not only did I bury the hurt of his death, I hid memories of him, sparing myself the pain of what I was missing. By reconnecting to my memories and to those of my brothers, the pain of loss resurfaced for what we had lost and what might have been. But the picture of Dad is now fuller and more complete, and for that I am grateful.

I thank my brothers for joining me in the acknowledgment of the fiftieth anniversary of Dad's death. It was the single most intimate exchange of stories that we ever shared, certainly the most about Dad. It felt like a true opening of a door long locked, only needing a simple question answered: "What do you remember about Dad?" The key was available to all of us and we finally used it. Because of his early death, our memories of him will never be extensive. It was good to share what we could.

FOLLOWING DAD'S FOOTSTEPS

TWENTY-TWO

Day One

Today, November 11, 2016, is Veterans Day—a most auspicious day, as they might say in India. In the past, this would have been a holiday of relative insignificance, limited to a brief acknowledgement of my father's and grandfather's service after hearing the morning news announcement of the day. Maybe a noting of the flags flying and photos of veterans in the paper. And possibly even a quick query as to why banks were closed. But this Veterans Day is different. It dawns in Guwahati, the largest town in the Assam State.

—From my diary of the trip

* * *

F EW EUROPEANS AND even fewer Americans visit this area of India, which is attached like an appendix to the far northeastern edge of the country. The mighty Brahmaputra River flows through the Assam Valley here from its Himalayan source, traveling eighteen hundred miles to its confluence with the Ganges. Along the way, it hosts national parks, endangered animals, tribal villages and ancient Hindu temples, as well as tea plantations by the score. All would have been worthy of a journey, but we were on a different mission, one that had been years in the making: to follow my dad's World War II footsteps from Plainview, Texas to Misamari, India. From this base in 1945, Dad flew his 150 missions over the Hump to Kunming, China.

To partially relive Dad's experience, I needed to witness the challenges of flying the Himalayas, the feel of living in one of the wettest places on earth and the wonder of experiencing cultures radically different from mine. But I was looking for more. How did this experience affect my father? What would he have learned from it? What would I learn from it? And just maybe I would find an answer to why he never talked about any of it.

At the small, regional airport in Guwahati, my husband and I awaited the arrival of the New Delhi flight of Mack and his wife, Jan. We have often traveled with them, mostly to foreign locations—southern Mexico, Guatemala, Ecuador, Chile and Argentina, for example—and were comfortable with our shared traveling habits. From eating requirements (open to all experiences) to the low luxury level needed in hotels (safe and clean is the minimum) to travel requirements (buses are fine) to alcohol (one drink a night always perfectly caps a day), we were most compatible.

Planning began more than a year in advance. Passports had to be sent off to two embassies, flights with six foreign airlines booked, connections and trips through the night had to be evaluated, and even a State Department warning against travel in the Assam Valley and Nagaland had to be weighed. My brother and I are not easily dissuaded from traveling. Our experience is that these warnings are overly cautious.

It is different with my husband. Despite having traveled through Europe after college and having explored Central and South America over the years, Ed is not an adventurous traveler. As a pediatrician, he can find lots to worry about. Whenever we approach a foreign country, we are heavily vaccinated, our carry-on medicines are ready to treat anything from diarrhea, asthma, pain and blisters to amoebas and infections, and we are always accompanied by a large supply of mosquito repellent.

At the top of the worry list for this trip was the eighteen hours of flying time to get to the Assam Valley. Because Ed's six-foot-three frame and his inability to sleep on a plane have made some journeys miserable, he didn't sign on quickly. We had to review weather, clean water availability, insects, waterborne diseases, the safety records of our airlines and the types of planes we would be flying. In the end, he did it for me. Ed was grateful to have had time with his father in the twilight of his life to learn about his father's war experiences, and he wanted me to get as close as I could to my Dad's war life.

Day one of our trip. Veterans Day, in the Assam Valley, India, 2016. With my husband, Ed, on the left and my brother and sister-in-law, Mack and Jan Walker.

An hour earlier, Ed and I had exited our Air India plane feeling dazed and wobbly from the hours of flying and disoriented by the twelve-hour time difference. The arrival hall was light and airy with high ceilings. Banners from the recent Diwali, or "Festival of Lights," warned against excessive candle-lighting, large photos of tigers advertised the nearby Kaziranga National Park, and photos of masked dancers beckoned all to join the celebration on Majuli Island for the Raas Festival. It was already different from any place we had traveled before.

As we passed the hour, we visited with our guide, Himangshu Pathak, and his business partner, Raj Bhattacharjee. They were young entrepreneurs who had begun their travel agency, NE Routes, just seven months earlier. Raj had seen my inquiry for guide services to track Dad's experience in India and was intrigued. We corresponded regularly in planning our trip and I found both men's suggestions helpful. Our itinerary included sites that would have been important to Dad's history, as well as many of the wonders available in that beautiful valley.

While we waited for Mack and Jan, we discussed what felt to be our most pressing problem: India had just recalled all thousand- and five-hundred-rupee bills and wasn't issuing any more. Only new bills could be used, but they weren't available yet. As a result, ATM machines stood empty, unable to provide any currency, causing us to wonder how we would get cash. Our guides assured us that everything would be fine, and it was.

Finally, Mack and Jan appeared at the top of the stairs with big smiles and moved toward us through the crowd. We embraced in wonder and relief that our rendezvous could happen on time, a half-world away from Texas. I couldn't stop smiling from a sense of initial accomplishment and for the excitement of the beginning of a trip long sought.

The journey that had brought us to this place had felt like a marathon, involving three planes, two customs stamps, twelve time zones and two middle-of-the-night flights. Yet it was nothing compared to the path my father had traveled. His trek to the Assam Valley seventy-one years earlier had taken months and had included stops in at least a dozen countries.

As I stood in the Guwahati airport on that Veterans Day, neither those seventy-one years nor the dramatic difference in our itineraries mattered. On that Veterans Day, I stood where he had stood, wishing we could salute each other but having to settle for a shared view. Despite the years since his death, his absence hurt.

TWENTY-THREE

The Misamari Base

"Charlie was stationed at Misamari... It was on the Brahmaputra River, quite a river, especially compared to the Mississippi. That river followed down the assigned valley and turned south at Misamari. We took off over the bend of the river. There was just one runway. We very seldom had much wind. The Himalayas started about four miles away, pretty high and rugged there, and cut off any wind except the wind that usually blew up and down the valley, parallel to the runway."

—Mont Jennings interview as corrected

* * *

I AWOKE THE morning of our scheduled visit to Misamari excited, alert and anxious, wondering whether the experience ahead would match my expectation. After our arrival in Guwahati, we spent two nights near Kaziranga National Park, where we rode elephants to search for one-horn rhinoceros and explored the park's abundant wildlife by jeep. It was an exciting introduction to the area but lacked any connection to our trip's purpose.

The first I knew of Dad's World War II location was from the Jennings interview. I remember pausing as I typed "Charlie was stationed at Misamari," the words pulled from Dad's past, landing in my present. Before we arrived, I could only imagine the place in India where Dad had been, despite Mont Jennings' description. Today, I would explore that small town in India that had a family connection with me. It held my father's spirit, along with those of hundreds of other pilots.

The drive from the park to the base began on a nicely paved highway. We passed farmers driving water buffalos in circles to break up the newly harvested rice crop, the same scene from one of my father's war photos. Other shared sights were women carrying baskets on their heads and men with fishing poles walking along the road. Soon we crossed the Brahmaputra River—finally, after having read about it for years. From Jennings' descriptions, I knew that Dad and other pilots would have used this river to confirm their location, particularly during takeoff and landing. It remains a major riverway, with large transport barges and smaller shallow draft boats moving slowly under the 1.8-mile-long bridge, a major addition since my father's time when no bridge crossed the wide river.

While many guidebooks are available for the Assam Valley, none mentions Misamari. The reason is simple. There is no real reason to visit the town except to connect with a seventy-one-year-old war experience. Although the town is still viable and continues to host an Indian air force base, its residents would be surprised that anyone would travel twelve thousand miles to visit it, probably because the base's war history is virtually ignored by its population. Himangshu was especially helpful, having visited the base twice before our arrival. Although he couldn't guarantee we would be allowed in, he was hopeful.

Soon after crossing the river, our driver, Dilip, chose a back road, supposedly better than the main route farther north. We passed soccer fields filled with adults and children playing, often with more than one game going. Tiny villages hosted neighborhood stores next to a school or a temple. Riders on motorcycles seemed to make better time on the pothole-filled road. Often, it was easier to move off the uneven paved area and onto the well-used dirt paths. Tea plantations were a constant presence, as they would have been in Dad's time. Dilip worked hard to find the smoothest route around the holes. Cars were rare.

On the outskirts of Misamari, a bar across the road stopped us and a soldier indicated that Himangshu should follow him. Himangshu gathered our passports and his papers to talk to a seated officer inside a nearby office. Without embarrassment, the remaining soldiers and locals stared at us. I was becoming used to the frank stares, a phenomenon our small

Misamari Control Tower, 1942.

American group generated wherever we went. I can imagine what the locals thought when thousands of soldiers landed in their midst during World War II, certainly a first introduction to Western men for most of them. Himangshu returned smiling. With a nod from the officer, the bar was raised, and we entered the town of Misamari. Himangshu warned us not to take photos when we got to the base.

After the war ended, this base was one that stayed open under Indian supervision. The military presence dominated the town itself, with many apartments and barracks. Other than the surrounding tea plantations and rice farms, little commercial activity seem to exist. The only real commercial presence in town was an outdoor market in the central area, where stalls overflowing with produce, meats, trinkets, cookware, clothes and shoes lined the streets—a kind of stretched-out Walmart.

We turned onto the road leading to the base. Its entry was just across the railroad tracks. I was strangely anxious that something would stop us after the many miles we had traveled to be here. Surprisingly, the original control tower from World War II was still there, preserved with a sign indicating its importance during the war. It was a thrill to see the tower that had been responsible for bringing Dad safely back to ground on his 150 missions, especially now knowing what the controllers had to keep track of: a steady stream of arriving flights circling above, only five hundred feet of altitude separating them, while giving takeoff instructions for the constant line of planes on the ground. Dad navigated it all, even in low-lying clouds.

"This building standing tall," the sign on the control tower read, "is the Air Traffic Control Tower constructed at Misamari Air Force Base during World War II as part of Hump Route Infrastructure. Numerous Flights which flew over the Hump route were efficiently directed by OPRS Round the Clock to maintain the supply being transferred to China by these aircraft. This ATC was closed by OPS after the Allied victory over the Japanese in 1945. Given the rich history and the major part played by Misamari base and its ATC tower it has now been converted into a heritage location to preserve and showcase the chequered history associated with it."

The use of the word "chequered" was surprisingly accurate if it was describing the progress of the Hump operation from its initial failures and dangers to a safer, more productive run in 1945. I smiled at the recognition of the base as having a "rich history" and playing a "major part" in the war, words I wanted to attribute to my father's efforts.

Next to the sign was a large black-and-white photo of a World War II American GI in shorts; he was shirtless, wearing combat boots and a bib hat. With hands on his hips, he stared confidently into the camera, comfortable in his environment, sans soldier's uniform or pilot's hat. We have similar photos of Dad dressed down in only Bermuda shorts and combat boots. The photo probably indicates the casualness associated with this hot, wet outpost on the other side of the world. On the tower itself, the elevation of 312 feet was posted in large letters, along with the tower's date of establishment, 1942.

To the left of the road was the original runway, now perfectly paved and enclosed in a high wire fence topped with barbwire. The runway's original steel mesh had been paved over. Across the runway were hangars that still had English names, such as Soldiers of the Sky. As we approached the entry gate, a large drone landed. When we stopped at a second bar across the road, Himangshu warned us again not to take pictures. I gave him copies of papers that showed that Dad had been posted in Misamari, along with some pictures of him. Himangshu disappeared into the office, hoping to persuade the officer in charge to allow us to enter.

We waited outside the van, standing in the back, taking in the view and sounds of air force activity. I had brought the description of the base from the Jennings interview and asked if everyone wanted to hear it. They did, and I began to read the interview, the words unveiling Dad's experience here. Images of thatched roof baches with monkeys scampering across came alive. Indian laborers appeared, loading planes with fuel. C-46s and C-47s lined up on the runway, ready to roar into action with Dad in one of them. We could almost see him moving to the steel-mesh runway, revving up the plane, checking the wind direction once last time and taking off, climbing quickly and disappearing into the clouds. Dad seemed so close that day, tearfully close.

After I finished, we stood still in the gentle wind, breathing in the Himalayan shadows. Dad had been here, in this very foreign location filled with sights and sounds different but not unfamiliar to a Texas Panhandle farm boy. His vista at home was also flat and endless, but with cotton and corn fields stretching in neatly planted sections. In India, tea plantations and rice fields served the same agricultural purpose, with tea bushes planted on hillsides and rice paddies near the water. Growing up, Dad had rudimentary tractors to help him and his brothers with seeding and harvesting. I'm confident he would have watched with interest the water buffalo used here for harvesting rice and the elephants used for transporting. We had experienced those same sights on the drive in to Misamari that day, passing a family harvesting their small plot of rice and guiding water buffalos in circles to break up the rice stalks. Mack had insisted we stop the car to talk with the family and to analyze their harvesting method. It reminded me of Dad's keen interest in how things worked, and I thought that he might have done the same thing on his time off.

Himangshu returned dejected. He couldn't talk the officer into allowing us in. The commanding officer was out of town and the acting commanding officer had his orders. Misamari is very close to China's border. After a

1962 war that the Indian army lost, the Indian military has stayed on perpetual high alert. There had been some skirmishes at the border with Nepal in recent days, and the acting CO couldn't allow the distraction of our presence on his base. The decision seemed excessive, but those were his instructions. It didn't matter how far we had come. The fact that we were children of a Hump pilot mattered little.

In fact, no one that I had yet met was impressed with my father's World War II history in India. I was just a foreigner visiting their country. If India had fought in World War II, it was because they were told to by the British. I would soon discover that the Chinese fought instead to protect their country. It made all the difference in how my brother and I were received in the two countries.

Sadly, I climbed back into the van. The disappointment was there but I hadn't come to see the workings of a modern Indian air force base. I had come to more fully understand Dad's experience in this remote location, and that we did. As we drove back past the historic control tower, I was grateful that I had seen the tower, runway and hangars and that I got to spend thoughtful time amongst the ghosts of the past.

Our final stop in Misamari was at the railroad station for a photo with the station sign indicating the town's name. In the 1940s, the base had had a railroad station of its own; that's where they unloaded the gasoline that came in by rail before it got reloaded onto the planes. We had to park some blocks out and walk past the central market spread out along the main street. From the stares and reaction of the vendors and shoppers, not many Americans come this way, at least not since the end of the war.

Mack and I stood under the Misamari sign, proud to be able to share this important part of Dad's life, wishing he were here to show us around, to point out what had changed and much that hadn't, to tell us funny stories of life in the war, to reminisce about a dangerous flight or a spectacularly beautiful one, to confess his homesickness, his bouts with diarrhea or malaria, or to rejoice in his remembered excitement as he neared the end of his tour. We would never have the details of his time here, but for this day it was enough to just be here, feeling his presence and that of many other soldiers, sharing an experience, and giving thanks for their service.

As we drove away, I realized that this first encounter with Dad's past had not been as emotionally wrenching as I had anticipated, just very satisfying. Thanks to our visit to the base, I could now envision his time in India. A void had been partially filled. And we still had Kunming ahead to fill in more of the puzzle.

With my brother Mack at the Misamari train station.

TWENTY-FOUR

Hump Connections

During World War II, the tribes in Nagaland were paid one hundred silver rupees by the Allies to bring in pilots who were forced to parachute out of an uncontrollable plane, the money acting as an incentive to protect the downed crew.

* * *

AN UNUSUAL TASK I had given myself on the trip was to seek out and thank the Nagaland people for their help in saving downed pilots during the war. They were a small but important connection to the Hump operation. Stories were told of pilots appearing at Ledo or Chabua in the Assam Valley weeks after they had been assumed dead, accompanied by native warriors. A good friend of mine shared a letter from her uncle written during the war detailing his experiences with the Naga people after he had to bail out of his plane over their lands. They provided him with successive guides who ultimately led him to an American base in the Assam Valley.

Fortunately, my father never needed their services, yet it was comforting to know that help would have been there had he needed it. These former headhunters had a fierce reputation a century and a half ago; today they are mostly Baptists—a transformation that shocks everyone I tell. Their conversion began in 1872 with the arrival of Baptist missionaries. It took many years for all the Naga tribes to convert, a process that continued during the World War II years. Every village we saw now had a Southern

Baptist-style church with an adjoining pastor's home.

Nagaland is its own separate Indian state, barely accessible by one of the worst roads of my traveling career. We arrived in Mon in the Naga Hills at night after eight hours on a pothole-filled road, making the final third of the drive in a dense fog. There were neither street signs nor street lights in the town of twenty-six thousand, and we had to back up more than once to find our hotel. The next morning was to be our excursion to Longa, a nearby village of the Konyak tribe.

The birds awakened us at 5:30 a.m., not long before a nearby radio began blasting a country and western song with English lyrics: "I got you. You got me. We got love." A solitary church bell rang, and soon a pig began rooting. With all that noise, it was easy to be up early and ready for the trip to Longa. At breakfast, we visited with a couple from England who were also in Nagaland to retrace a father's footsteps in World War II, an amazing coincidence that led to comparing stories over several cups of coffee.

The day before we had stopped at a liquor store for bottles of wine for the village chief. In exchange we would be given private time with him and his six elderly warriors, primarily to photograph a disappearing generation.

The ride to Longa was much easier than our trek to Mon had been. We arrived in thirty minutes and were taken to the village chief's home, where a group of elderly men sat in a semicircle around an open fire, their reddish smiles revealing their longtime use of the betel nut. Except for his gray synthetic polo shirt, the chief was dressed royally, wearing eight strands of large orange beads with four brass heads, each supposedly representing the head of a person killed by the warrior. The ends of small animal tusks disappeared into his elongated earlobes. He also wore large bone bracelets. The chief spelled his name in English for us: King Tuwing. Kota, the oldest of the men, was one hundred, while the king was the youngest at eighty-five. All were heavily tattooed on their faces and bodies with blood and vegetable dyes, a method that is no longer practiced.

Mack teased the chief, offering to exchange his safari hat for King Tuwing's wild bear turban with boars' teeth on the side. Bamboo formed the inside of the hat. All laughed at the inappropriateness of the swap. The feeling around the fire was companionable, even with the stark contrast in cultures.

Four wives joined the men and sat on a side bench, smiling readily. I noted their confidence and ease in wanting to be a part of the gathering.

Elders of the Konyak Tribe in Nagaland, India.

They wore coral bead necklaces with turquoise beads scattered in between. The chief's wife gently pulled up her skirt to reveal a tattoo just below her knee, a lace-looking ring around her leg. All the tattoos were fading as is the tradition. A young woman brought in three pineapples for us.

I had brought small pins with me from home, of an Eiffel tower topped with a red cowboy hat. When I travel, I often give them to people I meet, making me a kind of roving ambassador for Paris, Texas—the small town with the great name. As I slowly pinned one on each of the men's shirts, they laughed heartily. I wasn't sure whether they got the humor of the Texas cowboy hat atop the French Eiffel Tower or just thought it a funny thing to give them, or both. It all contributed to a cheerful ambiance.

With the aid of our interpreter, I told the king of my father's job as a Hump pilot and thanked his people for their help in saving some of our pilots and crew during World War II. Because of the advanced age of the men around the fire, they all would have been alive during the war years. The king nodded, whether in acknowledgement of their part in the war or simply to recognize I had spoken. I couldn't tell. He made no reply, not exactly the engaged response I had been hoping for, where we would admire each other's people and I would hear stories of pilots found. My offer of thanks was barely acknowledged, possibly because he had not been a part of that operation or because that is their way of receiving gratitude. I didn't press as the moment was already special.

As we left, Himangshu was very excited that we got to see the chief and elders, as they were not always available. Their generation is dying out and soon none will remain with the tribe's headhunter history. I felt the same about Dad's history; few remain to tell the story that was rapidly sinking until my journey began.

The connection with the Nagaland tribe was a planned encounter with the war's past in India, but I found two others. The first was an unexpected connection at the Wild Mahseer at Addabarie Tea Estate, a tea plantation converted into an ecolodge, with former employee bungalows now housing tourists. At dinner Richard and Jackie Leitch, the British host couple, were making the rounds of the French, German and American tourists visiting that night. Jackie approached our table, and when she learned the purpose of our trip, she excitedly called her husband over, knowing he was well-versed about the Hump operation and would want to talk to us. An inebriated Richard joined us and was astounded that he had American guests whose father had flown the Hump. He kept asking where we lived in the US and shaking his white mane in amazement. We were quickly invited to his home up the road for after-dinner drinks.

Richard grew up in the Assam Valley at this same tea plantation. He had deep roots in the British Raj era of India, including a great-uncle who was responsible for the development of the Indian rail system. He also had facts and stories to share: the number of Allied bases in the valley, the presence of an oil refinery in the Assam Valley that helped with the production of the gasoline being transported, the use of the runways after the war to deliver supplies during monsoon season. He remembered meeting a long, tall Texan in a cowboy hat in England who had flown the Hump and had more stories. To cap off the evening, a visiting professor specializing in elephants who had just been to Kunming assured us that we would be warmly welcomed in China. It was a special evening made possible by Dad's experience and our search.

Two nights later, we found our second unplanned wartime connection when we arrived at the large, eighty-seven-year-old Thengal Manor tea estate and discovered a previously unknown—at least to us—history from the Hump era: framed newspaper articles in the entry hall that talked about the 1940s meetings that had taken place at the plantation to discuss Indian independence. Even as my father and many other Hump pilots were taking off for China twenty-four hours a day less than sixty miles away in Misamari, the Barooak family, who still owned this historic home, were among the many educated Indians who were beginning to pay attention to Gandhi and his radical ideas of independence from Great Britain. This awakening was happening across India and is well-portrayed in The Jewel in the Crown series that aired on PBS years ago.

I doubt that my father would have been aware of the undercurrent of dissatisfaction Indians had toward the British. Since the Brits could require local tea plantations to give up some of their lands for air bases, Dad and the American government owed the British Empire for the success of his assignment. Today, allowing foreign troops on Indian soil would require intense negotiations with the Indian government. During the war, Great Britain and India had divergent goals. One was victory over China, the other victory over Great Britain. This could be another reason why the Assam Valley and India have chosen not to preserve or promote their part in the World War II story. It was only a blip on their crusade for independence.

TWENTY-FIVE

The Himalayas

The Himalayans are so close, their presence felt through the morning mist, a breathing, snow-covered sentinel hiding behind clouds. We are close to them in the Assam Valley, only twenty miles away. I try willing the mountains' appearance, staring hard through the white veil, but they refuse to play. They are shy, remaining shrouded during our visit.

—From my diary of the trip

* * *

L ONG BEFORE MY trip to India and China was planned, the world's highest mountains exerted a lure, a call to visit and admire. Tales from fellow travelers about Nepal's wonders brought a longing to trek, to experience views like no other. While I never considered serious mountain climbing, making it to base camp had seemed attainable. Now, however, there was a family connection to the range, a real reason to go—but not to Nepal. And trekking was not the goal; flying over the mountains was.

Wanting to physically retrace my father's route over the Himalayas into China, I searched extensively for a commercial flight that would fly from the Assam Valley into Kunming via Dad's Able course. None came close. I learned that the 1962 war between China and India had led to the closing of that airspace to commercial flights. To make our way to Kunming, we would have to return to Kolkata to take the only direct flight into Kunming, on Eastern China Airlines, a flight that left in the middle of the night. All other flights made lengthy stops in Bangladesh. While the flight would cover parts of Dad's route, it would be in the dark, with moonlight our only possibility of seeing the mountains.

I also had hoped to clearly see the Himalayas that lined the northern part of the Assam Valley. While monsoon season was over during my visit, hazy clouds still obscured the mountains. Occasionally, our guides would nod toward the north, pointing out a peaking mountaintop. With snow crowning their peaks and clouds covering the base, it was difficult to distinguish the mountain shape. I was frustrated at the end of our time in the Assam Valley, but I would have one more chance.

My last hope of experiencing the world's tallest mountains depended on our short jaunt to the Kingdom of Bhutan, a small neighboring country to the northeast of the Assam Valley that's nestled deep in the Himalayan range. Going there was Jan's idea. My sister-in-law and I both love indigenous cultures and we were excited about visiting this long-isolated country. While Bhutan and the Assam Valley share a border, we still had to return to Kolkata to travel back up to Bhutan on the only flights available into that sheltered country. We couldn't have traveled on a more beautiful day.

What I didn't know as we left Kolkata was that there were only twenty-five pilots qualified to land at Bhutan's Paro Airport. Nestled in the Himalayan mountains on the banks of the river Paro Chu, Paro is seventy-three hundred feet above sea level and is surrounded by peaks as high as eighteen thousand feet. The terrain is so unforgiving and the weather so severe at times that flights are allowed only under visual meteorological conditions and are restricted to daylight hours. That description was reminiscent of the difficult conditions flying the Hump, but pilots like my Dad had to fly regardless of weather.

As we approached Bhutan from Kolkata, the Himalayas grew, stretching in waves of first triangular peaks and later snowbound cones, six-deep in layers. I had never seen such depth of high mountains. They seemed endless. Too soon, the beautiful new dragon-painted Bhutan Airlines plane began its descent, bringing us close enough to scan zigzag dirt roads leading to isolated, ten-home villages, some perched on plateaus alongside fields of wheat, potatoes, buckwheat and barley.

As we dropped closer, the pilot followed the Paro Chu valley, and we saw increasing numbers of homes and fields as we approached the airport.

My view of the Himalayas from our Bhutan Airline flight, as we approached Bhutan from Kolkata, India.

Little time was available to our pilot to straighten the plane before he quickly landed on what seemed a short runway. Gratefully, I had not yet read that this is considered one of the world's most dangerous approaches for commercial airlines.

Hump pilots also used Himalaya valleys during their World War II flights, but under different conditions. Then, pilots needed valleys to decrease their altitude because of icing. Mountains would be surrounding them, even if they weren't visible. The crew could only hope that the fog would clear enough so that they would avoid flying into a mountainside or that the ice would melt quickly enough to allow the planes to ascend again. I'm sure Dad flew in both sunny days and stormy nights. While I will never experience his flying at night or in rain, I finally had his view on a clear day—one of the loveliest in all my travels. He must have been in awe, even after 150 trips. I know I was.

TWENTY-SIX

Happy Jack, Our Driver

"Thank you for your father's service."
—Jack, our Chinese driver in Kunming

* * *

W E HAD EXPECTED our Chinese guide Elena to meet us at Kunming's Changshui International Airport, a beautiful facility just
opened in 2012. I had found her through an internet search. She worked
independently rather than through a guide service and came with good re-
views. What we hadn't expected was Jack, our driver.

Jack smiled as much as Elena didn't. He was a happy guy and loved his
English name. He had just bought a used Mercedes van to get back into
the tourist industry. Some years earlier, when his father had needed help
on the family farm, Jack left his job as a driver and returned home. Unfortunately, the farm couldn't turn the profit needed to support two families
and had to be sold. Jack's parents then moved in with him, his wife and
their son. Jack was now the only one working in his family, and we were
one of his first clients.

Our first stop was at the Stone Forest, a petrified-rock outcropping with
trails up, over and through the massive stones. It's been gentrified for the
masses of Chinese that are now traveling in their own country, with easy
transportation to the forest and paved trails throughout. Elena asked Jack
to be our guide there as she seldom came to the Stone Forest and he knew

Happy Jack giving us the "thumbs-up."

more about it. We patiently listened to his recounting of the forest's history. Jack's English was good, if a bit stiff, and I learned not to interrupt him with a comment or observation, as he had to stay on his internal script.

It was only on the ride to the hotel that Jack discovered the purpose of our trip; Elena had not told him. He couldn't believe it. Our father had flown the Hump? He was honored to be in our presence and kept repeating, "Thank you for his service." His response was the first indication that we would be treated differently in China than we had been in India.

Throughout our time in Kunming, Jack was eager to learn more about Dad's experiences. He spent as much time in the museums as we did, carefully reading each display and often making observations when we returned to the van. For example, he told us that most Chinese did not distinguish the pilots who flew the Hump from the Flying Tigers, a civilian air force led by Claire Lee Chennault of Texas. The Flying Tigers were the first pilots to take on the Japanese and win in China. The Chinese people merged the Flying Tiger pilots and Hump pilots together in their respect for the World War II effort. Jack was happy to learn the difference and to discover how dangerous Hump flying had really been. Every time he learned something new about the Hump missions, he would repeat, "Thank you for your father's service."

TWENTY-SEVEN

The Hump Restaurant

"You and your children are always welcome here."

—Mr. Wong, manager of the
Hump Restaurant in Kunming

* * *

BEFORE WE ARRIVED in Kunming, Elena had alerted us to a restaurant called The Hump. She had previously made a special trip to visit Mr. Wong, its manager, and he had agreed to talk with us about the restaurant's history. We were due there on our second day in Kunming, but because of heavy downtown traffic, we were running late and had to hurry across the large Jinbi Plaza that was anchored by the two remaining original entry gates into the city. I thought of Dad passing through either the Golden Horse Gate or the Jade Rooster Gate when he had visited the old city of Kunming, and I was envious that he got to see it before all the development.

Strangely, the facade of the restaurant reminded me more of an English tearoom than anything military, with its white-shuttered windows, tied curtains and window boxes. Only a sign above an airplane propeller attached to the outside wall reading "The Hump since 2000" and globe lights outlining the Hump flight pattern over silhouetted mountains revealed its true focus. I was astounded to find this gem in a corner of downtown Kunming, with crowds of young Chinese hurrying by, faces buried in cellphones, uninterested in the historical significance of this restaurant.

Mr. Wong (I never learned his first name) sat in a darkened corner of the café, a burning cigarette in hand, like a scene out of a 1940s movie. He looked older than his forty-three years, his face wrinkled from years of chain smoking. Smiling but stooped, he rose to acknowledge us and motioned for us to sit down, offering coffee drinks such as cappuccinos and lattes, a first on our Chinese visit. After years of greeting other veterans and their families, including a ninety-two-year old ex-pilot, Wong's English was fluent and his knowledge of the Hump operation in Kunming extensive.

I was curious about the restaurant's history. Wong told us that its founder, Sun Haibo, had opened it in 2000 to memorialize and honor the pilots who had flown the Hump. Sun now lives outside China because of his dislike of the Communist Party, which defeated Chiang Kai-shek after World War II. As president of the organization that owns the restaurant, Sun brought in ten Hump veterans to tell their stories when the restaurant opened.

Wong had his own small personal history with the war. His father's family was bombed in Kunming by the Japanese and his father remembers running from the Japanese when their airplanes approached. His family was one of many who were saved by the appearance of Chennault and the Flying Tigers and who were then kept alive by the Hump operation.

According to Wong, Wujaiba, Kunming's original airport, was the second one built in all of China. Kunming would have been a nice size town during the war, with a population of three hundred thousand in the 1940s. It has since grown to seven million. Wong acknowledged that few Chinese know about the airport's historical significance in World War II or about the Hump operation, but that most are familiar with the Flying Tigers. He told us that there's some in official history books about the operation but that it is mostly being passed down orally and in museums. Even so, China's previous leader, Hu Jintao, invited Hump pilots to Beijing to be honored, a sign that the Communists have begun to accept this part of their history, even though it includes Chiang Kai-shek. Chennault and his Chinese wife, however, have long been accepted and recognized in China, and their family home in Kunming is another restaurant, the Flying Tigers, which we would also visit during our stay.

I learned from Wong that just the month before, Tom Clayton, wearing a Chinese National Air Corps (CNAC) insignia on his jacket, flew a seventy-two-year-old C-47 from Burma into the new Kunming airport; it

With my brother Mack and Mr. Wong at the Hump Restaurant in Kunming.

was destined for a Flying Tiger museum in Guilin, east of Kunming. He did not fly the Hump path because of worries about the plane's durability after so many years. There was comprehensive media coverage for the flight, and although I didn't know it at the time, that event would later help me find a veteran Hump pilot in Australia.

The cafe was a mini-museum, filled with authentic memorabilia from World War II, including a flight jacket with Chinese words sewn inside it to indicate that the pilot was a good guy and to instruct any peasants who found him to take care of him. The bold painting on the wall was of the wartime pilot lingo *ding hao*, which means "good job" or "thumbs up" and which was often painted on Flying Tigers' aircraft. On the ceiling was a large model of a Flying Tiger plane and a map that I had seen on the internet of the Hump's main towns. Old photos of a C-47 flying over a peasant's home and that of a traditional Chinese family were displayed, and paintings of black silhouetted camels on the wall mimicked those painted on the Hump planes, indicating a completed trip over the Himalayas. *Tuo Feng* means "camel peaks" in Chinese, which is where the name "the Hump" comes from. Ever hopeful, I scanned the photos of pilots for a glimpse of Dad. Unfortunately, he wasn't in any of them. Still, I couldn't get enough of those now-familiar items in this foreign land.

That day, most of the restaurant clientele was young, drinking late-afternoon coffees and seemingly oblivious to the significance of their surroundings. Wong confirmed that this was the usual crowd at The Hump. As well, he said, the restaurant often features a band and serves liquor in addition to coffee drinks. Part of me wanted to engage with one table of smiling youth, to point out the meaning of the memorabilia and to tell them how special the restaurant was, that there was more to it than just good coffee and music.

I admired the brown cotton apron worn by one of the waitresses; it simply had the word "Hump" in English, along with its Chinese translation, *Tuo Feng*. I wanted to buy one and looked around for a gift store. But Wong wouldn't let me pay and insisted on giving me one as a gift. He instructed the waitress to give me hers, covered with stains as it was. The waitress hesitated as she knew it was soiled. Wong nodded to her that it was okay and said to us, "Your father helped our country." I teared up at the unexpected offer, an acknowledgement that my father's special work lives on and is appreciated. Today, when I look at the apron, it brings back many memories of our trip and of all that I've learned about Dad and the Hump—the Chinese and English words connecting both the war operation and the two countries. I love this apron.

Surprisingly, Wong had never been to the Kunming monument honoring Hump pilots. He did, however, ask for pictures or anything else we had on Dad's time as a Hump pilot. We exchanged emails, even though Gmail and Google are not available in China.

"You are always welcome," he assured us, "and your children."

As Wong walked us out of the cafe, our education continued as he explained that the propeller on the outside of the building was from a

A wall in the Hump Restaurant in Kunming. *Ding Hao* was WWII pilot lingo meaning either "thumbs up" or "good job."

Russian plane. It had four propellers; an American plane would have had only three.

We said goodbye to this small man who anchors a restaurant's effort to acknowledge a much larger Hump history in Kunming. I was amazed that it survives amongst the city's building explosion but grateful for the owner's and manager's determination to keep the story alive. I hope it will be there for years to come for other descendants of Hump pilots to visit.

Waitress at the Hump restaurant with the apron gifted to me by the manager in recognition of my father's role in WWII.

TWENTY-EIGHT

The Flying Tigers:
Then and Now

Bright lights flash Chinese lettering outside the Flying Tigers Restaurant, a welcome sight in the winter rain. In the dark space above, a second sign, "Flying Tigers Restaurant," welcomes English speakers. The restaurant's entryway leads into a long hall lined with memorabilia from Claire Lee Chennault's time in Kunming. The Flying Tigers Restaurant is in the home Chennault lived in after the war with his Chinese wife, Anna. Photos of his war days and of his postwar family life provide a visual contrast of his time in China: a time of both war and peace. A wedding picture of Chennault and Anna, in a white gown rather than the traditional Chinese red, documents the assimilation of each into the other's culture.

The large dining room rises dramatically up three stories, with a large-scale model of a P-40 hanging from the ceiling. More photos fill niches along one wall. Waitstaff are dressed in olive green jackets with a bowtie and a winged insignia over the breast pocket, meant to resemble a World War II pilot's uniform but succeeding only in making them look like enlistees of the Chinese army.

* * *

Truthfully, prior to this journey to reconnect with my father, I knew more about the Flying Tigers than I did about flying the Hump. In the early 1970s, I read *Stillwell and the American Experience in China* by Barbara Tuchman, which won the Pulitzer Prize at the time. I can't remember if I chose to read it because of Tuchman's reputation or because it won the Pulitzer or, possibly, because I harbored some hope of learning something about Dad's experience in China. Regardless, it is an excellent book and introduced me to the Flying Tigers. The group commands legendary fame, both in the United States and, particularly, in China.

At the beginning of the war, China had fewer than seventy-five planes that were operational. Madame Chiang Kai-shek knew that China had to be brought into the modern world to survive. As wife of Generalissimo Chiang Kai-Shek, she was in a position to import an American Volunteer Group (AVG) that became known as the Flying Tigers.

The Flying Tigers was originally a civilian air force, organized secretly in the United States with the help of the Chinese and British to prepare to fight the Japanese, should that become necessary. It was a mercenary group of pilots and flight crew, trained in Burma before the war started, and under the leadership of Claire Lee Chennault, a Texan from Commerce, only forty miles from where I live.

The Flying Tigers prided themselves on their unconventional, quick-attack approach to fighting, a stark contrast to Chinese timidity. Chennault was savvy in the Japanese "method" of attack, which, he knew, followed certain rules. Using that knowledge, Chennault developed a "strike-and-break-away" guerrilla technique for his P-40s. Because of the rules they were trained to obey, Japanese pilots couldn't respond in kind, despite their dominant numbers and greater maneuverability.

What also gave Chennault an advantage was a warning system called "*jing bao*," which was an organic effort by Chinese peasants on the ground to alert the Flying Tigers when the Japanese were approaching. Thanks to the telephones, telegraph and radios warning him of an air raid, Chennault was able to surprise the Japanese.

This joint effort, combining the people of China with the airpower of America, bound the two countries together early in the war. There would be many other instances—such as building airfields and roads rock by rock, driving trucks to deliver supplies and sheltering American pilots— that made the war effort a joint one. It also explains the positive feelings that western China has, even today, toward America and toward its World

War II contribution to fighting the Japanese. Our guide, Elena, noted that there were no ill feelings toward America in China. If the Chinese had an enemy still, she said, it would be Japan.

In modern-day Kunming, the Flying Tigers are considered to have been the saviors of the city during World War II. With the Pacific coast under Japanese control, Japan was free to attack the western half of China. Daily bombings out of Hanoi were taking a toll on Kunming because China's air force was not able to respond.

By 1941 Chennault had moved most of his planes and pilots to Kunming, and on December 20 at 10:00 a.m., a formation of ten Japanese Mitsubishis confidently flew toward the city for a routine bombing, unaware of any possible defense. Chennault had been forewarned and had seventeen P-40s in the air waiting for the Japanese. Using their strike-and-break-away tactic, the Flying Tigers attacked, taking down four bombers and sending the rest back damaged. It was the first time Kunming had been protected. The victory made world news at a time when good news was precious. And it began a special relationship between the Flying Tigers and the people of Kunming.

The pilots painted shark's teeth in a blood-red mouth and an evil eye on the noses of their planes. Inland Chinese had never seen a shark and thought the mouth of teeth looked like a tiger. The Chinese were so taken by Chennault's small air force that they named it, "*Fei-Hu*" or Flying Tigers, from a Chinese proverb: "Like tigers plus wings, their strength is irresistible." The name itself was irresistible, and what should have been called the American Volunteer Group became an almost mythical force: the Flying Tigers.

Unfortunately, the Flying Tigers couldn't sustain their victories across such a large area. They were vastly outnumbered by the Japanese, their assignments from the Chinese became impossible, and the force was disbanded in 1942 once contracts for the volunteers ended.

In Kunming today, America's assistance to China during World War II is taught in schools, so the Flying Tigers story is well known. In both the local and regional museums, large areas are dedicated to their efforts to protect Kunming. That is why the flashing sign over the Flying Tigers Restaurant wasn't such a surprise to me and why we decided to enter one evening.

As we had done with every unheated restaurant in Kunming, we searched for a corner away from the cold draft coming in from the open door. And as at every restaurant in Kunming, we hoped for a waiter or guest who spoke some English. No other Westerners were dining there that night and the maître d' was the only one who knew any English, although it was just a smattering. But he knew enough to be concerned when we ordered a bottle of wine, by far the most expensive liquor on the menu. Mack had to pay for the bottle before they would open it.

By this time, we were attracting attention from guests and from the line of waiters who came over to stare at us. My brother and I felt obliged to identify ourselves as the children of a Hump pilot and tried our best to distinguish that operation from the Flying Tigers. The maître d' indicated an understanding and mimed a plane flying and guns being shot. We shook our heads no and tried to become pilots flying over large mountains. He nodded blankly. We then smiled at each other, recognizing that the communication had failed. The waiters wandered away and we were left to inspect our food, ordered by pointing to pictures.

The restaurant experience bolstered our driver's observation that most Chinese group together the Flying Tigers with the Hump pilots who carried supplies over the Himalayas. Still, having a successful restaurant in Kunming named after an American/Chinese venture felt good, even if it wasn't a part of Dad's life.

Three of the waiters at the Flying Tigers Restaurant in Kunming.

TWENTY-NINE

Kunming Day: Finding Its World War II History

A cleaning woman is sweeping the floor of the World War II exhibit in the Kunming City Museum, her young child in tow. The girl is cheerful and energetic as she pushes a child-size broom. I wonder if her mother has even looked at the war display detailing the Hump's operation, and I wonder what she would think about my father's presence in Kunming all those years ago.

I want to talk to her. I want to tell her my story, my dad's story. I want her to know I have a connection to her country. Our people once fought together. I want her to know that I'm not just a tourist passing through. But the language barrier is too great and my thoughts too complicated for a pantomime. Instead, all I do is smile at her child and play peekaboo with her.

—From my diary of the trip

* * *

THURSDAY MORNING BEGAN in a chilly fog, typical for November in Kunming. A bit of anxiety and excitement hovered over the breakfast table. Today was the day—our *raison d'être* in Kunming. We were to explore the city's acknowledgment of the importance of the Hump operation and the last of its vestiges. I wanted it to be a catharsis, a revelation, a connection to Dad, but I feared my expectations were too high.

Elena wanted to start at the Kunming City Museum with the section dedicated to the Flying Tigers and the Hump operation. The museum opened in 2014 and the gray modern exterior masked its rich interior. As in most of Kunming, there was no inside heat, but at least we were sheltered from the light rain. A sign pointed to the American Volunteer Group Memorial Hall next to the Dinosaur Fossil Exhibition. I hurried up a large stairway with an airplane suspended over it. Expecting a display or two, I was startled by room after room of war memorabilia that included photos and details of the Allied presence in Kunming during the war.

Because the Chinese in Kunming are primarily familiar with the Flying Tigers, most of the displays were about them. Claire Lee Chennault was given much attention, including a video that touched on his life both during and after the war. The dedication to him read: "During his time in China, Chennault led his troops with a fearless and tenacious fighting spirit using superb air combat tactics which had great successes against Japanese forces. He made a great contribution to the Chinese people with victory of the Anti-Japanese War and the Anti-fascist War." I wondered if the people back home in nearby Commerce, Texas, were aware of the recognition given by the Chinese to their native son.

Toward the end of this section were displays related to those who flew the Hump. I was moved by the obvious importance of this operation to the Chinese and by the fact that they would consider it important enough to give it a prominent position in their local museum. Smiling inwardly, I began to explore.

The memorabilia was surprisingly extensive. A parachute survival kit included a watch, knife, needle pliers, an AAF stereoscope used for map reading, an AAF Hump pilot map, a survival book for the jungle and a first aid packet—equipment that would have helped a downed pilot walk the thin line between life and death. At least Dad would have had a fighting chance to survive had he needed to bail out. Available to pilots were pocket guides to India, China and Burma as well as Chinese and Japanese language guides—a wartime nod to the visiting GIs. As curious as Dad was, I know he would have read through the guides and maybe learned a Chinese phrase or two.

The displays included photos of pilots arriving in Kunming, of their heavy loads of gasoline being offloaded by small Chinese men and of a C-47 in the air. A large map with bold red arrows indicating the Hump route from Chabua, India to Kunming was now very familiar to me. And *Instrument Flying Advanced*, a small booklet from Altus Army Air Field in Altus, Oklahoma and probably left behind by a young pilot, connected me back home.

Our reception in China had already been so different from India, where our presence was shrugged off. No museum in the Assam Valley told the Hump story. No restaurant carried the name of the operation there. No driver thanked us profusely for our father's service. Every acknowledgment of the importance of my father's work in World War II by China helped me understand what he had been through and the respect he deserved. I was experiencing his recognition by proxy, without any input from him. It felt unbalanced without his personal story, but it was unavoidable.

The day before Jan had asked Elena about visiting Wujaiba. The old Kunming airport was in the process of being demolished, having already been replaced by the one where we had arrived. Built in 1923, it had a long history, including my father's time there, a history that was about to

Map of the Hump flight course in Kunming Museum.

be covered over. Neither Jack or Elena knew if we could get in but both agreed to try.

Wujaiba was enclosed by tall prison-like walls, with a few entry points for construction crews. I could hear demolition balls crashing as we neared. Jack simply drove in through one of the entry points, waving at the guard station as we passed. Laughing like schoolchildren who had run away from the principal, we boldly drove over the paved area. The airport had only one main runway, the one Dad would have landed on. Some but not all the runway had already been torn up. We stopped toward the middle of the huge facility to examine the exposed strata of what remained of the runway, realizing that the bottom layer was made from compacted stones laid by hand by coolies, men and women of all ages. A takeoff during the war always had the possibility of rock damage to the props. Above the rocks were layers of reinforced concrete and asphalt.

The 360-degree view here would have been Dad's as he flew over the Yuang Mountains and over Lake Dianchi, lining up to land on the single runway. He would have parked with hundreds of other aircraft, which would have been quickly swarmed by locals unloading the plane. While that was going on and while the plane was being reloaded with whatever needed to be returned to India, Dad would have had some time to rest, play cards, talk weather with other pilots and eat. Since Dad ate eggs every morning of his life back home and eggs were available in China but not in India, he had to have been excited about that option. Hours later, when his plane was loaded for the return trip, Dad and his crew would have taken off for Misamari, regardless of the time of day or night.

Kunming, an ancient trading town that was bustling during the war, would have welcomed my father when he had extra time. The beautiful Chinese wooden structures were then intact, unlike when we were there, by which time most had been destroyed. As I had just learned from the Kunming City Museum, Dad would probably have seen posters advertising hostels available to servicemen for a dollar a night, a price that included full board, laundry, a haircut, Chinese study, a social club, opera, religious activity, Chinese official contact and medical care. I appreciated the effort made by the people of Kunming to welcome our foreign army.

As Mack and I stood on the runway for a photo, I spent a few minutes taking in the same 360-degree open view that Dad would have seen, realizing that the space would soon be filled with the ubiquitous Chinese apartment and commercial buildings. The location was prime, only two and half miles from downtown, and rents would be high. This had been an unexpected opportunity to share my father's expansive view—a familiar one to him and now to me—before it disappeared forever. I thanked Jack for bringing us here and we turned back to town for a visit to the Hump Monument.

With Mack at the old runway at Kunming's first airport.

THIRTY

The Hump Monument at Last

"In the international anti-fascist struggle during World War II from 1942-1945, Sino-American soldiers and civilians jointly opened an air route from Assam, India, to Kunming, China. It was through this airborne transport the Over-the-Hump flight over the Himalayas was accomplished.

"The monument is thereby erected by the Yunnan Province Committee of the Chinese People's Political Consultative Conference to commemorate this daring feat in the history of aviation and the friendship between Sino-American soldiers and civilians fighting shoulder-to-shoulder in the anti-fascist battle to cherish the value of world peace, to recall the martyrs, to commend the survivors, and to inspire posterity. Always cherish the memory of the Over-the-Hump Flight."

—Inscription near the Hump Monument in Kunming, China.

* * *

IT WAS THE stillness I noticed first. In a city of seven million people, no one else was near. The clouds had cleared, and blue sky contrasted with evergreen woods. Halfway up a mountainside in Jiaoye Park, the Hump Monument shone through the surrounding forest.

Jack could only take us so far in the van. When he stopped at the end of the road, we climbed out and looked up a steep, three-flight staircase to the part of China dedicated solely to the Hump operation, a huge headstone

The Hump Monument, located in Jiaoye Park, Kunming, China.

in the forest. I had been anticipating this moment since I first learned of its existence and I wanted to savor every second, note every detail, capture internally this expression of respect for Dad's work. I had seen photos of the monument on the internet that accurately reflected the structure, but they couldn't capture the beauty of the setting. Tears hovered but didn't spill over yet, as at the beginning of a child's wedding.

The monument was dedicated in 1993 at a time when the government was secure enough to recognize the Allied role in saving China during World War II, even if it also included the anti-communist Chiang Kai-shek's history. Veteran Hump pilots were flown in to talk, while international news media covered the event. Through the next years, other gatherings of pilots here have recognized the operation, including a seventieth anniversary ceremony in March 2012.

Two-thirds of the way up the stairs, we stopped to catch our breath at a three-part outdoor display that detailed the Hump history in English and Mandarin. The pictures were faded from the sun and the glass dirty, but the story was well-written, with facts and figures and with an impressive, flowery acknowledgement of the deed. By now I knew many of the details it listed about the operation—flying over mountains at fifteen thousand feet or higher, navigating between snow-covered peaks and valleys, suffering through "extremely inclement" weather of rough winds, hailstorms, low air pressure and frost. The language itself was extravagant, describing the trip along "The Fatal Air Route" and a "treacherous route."

Also in the display was an acknowledgement of the part the Chinese people played in the Hump operation. As a part of the Chinese War of Resistance against the Japanese, an army of over one million Yunnan workers built ten new airfields in Yunnan Province, turning the area into one huge construction site. "Never before in Yunnan's history had there been a grand spectacle like this one." Photos of this operation showed the rock of the airfields being crushed under large concrete rollers pulled and pushed by individual Chinese, not by machines. It was a reminder of the combined efforts in the air and on the ground that were needed for the Hump operation to be successful.

I moved to the top, my chest tightened with emotion even as I didn't know what to expect. I had traveled thousands of miles for this—a monument dedicated to my father and to the thousands of other pilots who had faced down death daily. I looked at Mack, thinking of all that we had gone through together since Dad's early death, how he had believed in this journey, and how grateful I was that he was there too. He appeared as touched by the majesty of the setting as I was.

Much thought had gone into the design of the monument, built of white marble: the outline of a plane merging with two mountaintops, with the suggestion of a large H blended in. Three layers of meaning emerged: The H stood for the Hump, the mountains reflected the Himalayas and a plane represented the transport. Part of the monument formed a bridge between the two sides that one could walk through and around. I did both.

Some of the marble blocks appeared to have loosened, causing inward tilts of the stone. Mildew and dirt had formed in corners. Two standing wreaths, their flowers dead and their ribbons faded, stood on each side of the walkway up—possibly remaining from the recent pilot's event. A layer of neglect hung over the space even as its importance remained, true of some war memorials even in the States. Its condition didn't affect my appreciation for the effort to recognize the Hump operation, although I feared that its survival could be tenuous, with future generations of young Chinese more and more removed from the war.

Thoughtfully, Elena picked some bright yellow flowers from nearby bushes and asked if we wanted to put some in the wreath. The wording on the ribbon read, "Salute to the Chinese and American Soldiers and People who sacrificed during World War II." We threaded the live flowers with the dead, using the wreath as a grave marker as at the end of a funeral, each of us saying our own private prayer. Ed placed his arm around me as I fought back tears, swallowing hard, hampered by my emotional restraint. I couldn't cry then. That would come later when I was alone, as it always did. For now, all the work, the planning, the research and the stories came together on this beautiful winter afternoon with a powerful acknowledgement of their importance. My father had been a part of something significant. It was that simple and that profound.

Behind the monument, a separate marble structure contained a beautiful tribute, written by the Beijing Aviators Association and the Kunming Aviators Association; its plaque is quoted at the beginning of this chapter. I read it carefully.

Not once before had I considered my father as part of the international antifascist struggle. It was a vocabulary seldom used in the West, but one that is still an integral part of the communist world view. He had been honored by a very communist-sounding Yunnan Province Committee of the Chinese People's Political Consultative Conference. But he also had been recognized as a part of a "daring feat in the history of aviation" and as

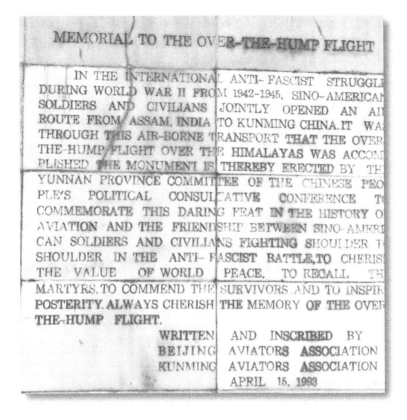

MEMORIAL TO THE OVER-THE-HUMP FLIGHT

IN THE INTERNATIONAL ANTI- FASCIST STRUGGLE DURING WORLD WAR II FROM 1942-1945, SINO-AMERICAN SOLDIERS AND CIVILIANS JOINTLY OPENED AN AIR ROUTE FROM ASSAM, INDIA TO KUNMING CHINA. IT WAS THROUGH THIS AIR-BORNE TRANSPORT THAT THE OVER THE-HUMP FLIGHT OVER THE HIMALAYAS WAS ACCOM PLISHED THE MONUMENT IS THEREBY ERECTED BY TH YUNNAN PROVINCE COMMITTEE OF THE CHINESE PEO PLE'S POLITICAL CONSULTATIVE CONFERENCE T COMMEMORATE THIS DARING FEAT IN THE HISTORY O AVIATION AND THE FRIENDSHIP BETWEEN SINO-AMERI CAN SOLDIERS AND CIVILIANS FIGHTING SHOULDER T SHOULDER IN THE ANTI- FASCIST BATTLE,TO CHERIS THE VALUE OF WORLD PEACE, TO RECALL TH MARTYRS,TO COMMEND THE SURVIVORS AND TO INSPIR POSTERITY. ALWAYS CHERISH THE MEMORY OF THE OVER THE-HUMP FLIGHT.

WRITTEN AND INSCRIBED BY
BEIJING AVIATORS ASSOCIATION
KUNMING AVIATORS ASSOCIATION
APRIL 15, 1993

The Hump Monument dedication.

having worked side-by-side with the Chinese. I loved the poetic ending calling for world peace and inspiring posterity, the use of the word martyr to describe the dead and the most personal of all "to commend the survivors."

Elena and Jack read every word on every display and monument, Jack continuing to be the more enthusiastic. He even insisted on being in some of our photos. We began with a picture of Mack and me together, his hand resting on my shoulder in solidarity, then we added Jan and Ed, smiling in satisfaction at a goal achieved, and we completed the series with Jack in the middle, standing proudly with the two families of a Hump pilot. He said, again, as he had on numerous occasions, "Thank you. Thank you to the Americans. You helped us a lot."

Mack looked up after the pictures were taken and asked, "Do you hear the plane?"

I did—a light rumbling overhead. Glancing up, I saw a distant plane with vapors trailing behind it in the deep blue sky. "How appropriate is that?" I noted, both of us recognizing an imagined salute to Dad, his own personal flyover at this long-delayed memorial service. The plane that day would have been unrecognizable to my father, but the view familiar—a connection of the past with the present.

Dad's love of flying had led him to do his part in the Hump operation and it continued to play a large part in his life and ours after the war. It had also led us here to find a missing father, the thread that began and ended this journey. The view from above connected us. Different times but same trip, the same landing in a foreign land, the same sense of accomplishment in arriving.

Mack then turned to me again and observed, "I think we've honored Dad today by coming here." We had, indeed. We and all the country of China had commended our father. Smiling, I nodded in relief, a sense of peace and satisfaction releasing the emotional tension of the visit. Dad's presence had been all around us that day—within the museum, at the airport, in the mountains and now in the sky. I felt closer to him in this foreign country in death than in life.

The questions were still there and always would be. Answers lay behind an "infinite and unyielding" wall, as I once read about death. But Dad's aviation past was no longer completely in the shadows. He was front and center that day. He had landed in my present.

Afterword

THE DECISION TO follow my father's World War II experience in India and China led me down a more complicated path than just a foreign visit. In preparing for the trip, I was required to relive my time with him as a father, to experience anew his death and to pry open my brothers' memories and my own. The pain of and resentment for his absence resurfaced and subsided as I progressed. Taking the time in quiet settings to just meditate on my father allowed memories to surface of travel, of Christmas and of home life. The meditative silence was not an absence of noise but an opening to Dad's presence.

Research was frustrating. Dad's World War II records had burned in a fire in Washington, D.C. The pilot he had flown with over the Himalayas had died. And Mom's dementia prevented any meaningful discussion about Dad or his World War II experience. Research on his flying buddies and friends in Plainview resulted in the reading of many obituaries. I was too late for most first-hand sources.

While at times frustrating in its dead ends, the search was as close to a treasure hunt as I will experience, with pearls appearing in unexpected places: rejoicing over Dad's handwritten letter to my uncle…confirming Dad's presence in Misamari…discovering those holiday menus in Africa… drafting his timeline in the military…and, most importantly, finding a pilot who actually flew with him.

The thrill of the chase came with each new bit of information, minor though it might be. The discovery of Dad's World War II trunk, especially the letters from his student pilots, was like winning the jackpot. In those missives, a playful and competent personality emerged. I got a glimpse of his love life through a previously unknown girlfriend's poem and photo, complicating my view of Dad's later relationship with my mother.

Layered over the military treasures were new stories about his past, a gradual coloring-in of his personality. Cousins, an aunt and friends were quizzed for the first time about their impressions of Dad, revealing qualities that hadn't been apparent to his children. I have now discovered unexpected characteristics of Dad within my own personality. Most of those interviewed had stories of flying with my father.

My fading memory of him began to sharpen, with old and new stories coloring in his personality and experiences. I pulled him out of the deep waters of my mind, rescuing the memories. Discovering the "fun" side of Dad took some time, but it was there. He was no longer a taciturn father who was often absent. He was a real soldier, a real father and a real husband.

The fifth stage of grief is letting go. My experience felt more a welcoming back, an emerging from the shadows. I could let go of the belief that I didn't know my father. With Dad's fuller life safely tucked into my emotional memory, he now accompanies me with my mother, whose memories used to dominate my childhood reflections. I'm enjoying having my father in my life again. I like thinking about him now. He is clearer in death in my adulthood than he was when he was alive in my childhood.

The journey to physically follow his World War II footsteps couldn't bring actual stories of Dad, but it could and did allow me to recreate some of his experiences. From reading the personal accounts of pilots who flew over the Himalayas, I knew what he would have faced in the air. From the Hump's history, I learned about the immensity of the operation and its importance. Then on the ground in India, I saw what he would have seen. The foreignness of the living conditions was still there: elephants on the side of the road, monkeys chasing each other across roofs, tea plantations and steady rain. Despite China's modernization, I had his view of the mountains and lakes as he landed on the welcoming plateau of Kunming. And the recognition of the Chinese people and government for Dad's service was an unexpected and touching experience. I didn't discover why he never talked about his life in India and China, but his time there is no longer a mystery.

* * *

On our last day in China, Elena had other commitments and Mack and Jan were leaving on an earlier flight than we were. After Jack took them to the airport, he returned to drive Ed and me to a regional museum and to an old restored village. The regional museum also had an exhibit on Flying the Hump, in the room just before the one with displays about Mao's take-over of China. Jack continued to educate himself everywhere we went.

Then it was time to leave. On the drive to the airport, Jack said there was something he wanted to say to us. He had been struggling, he said, to express how he felt about my father. He just couldn't get the right trans-lation. But he kept trying and asking for help and now he knew. He said, "Your father was a hero." He said it twice. "Your father was a hero. That's what I've been trying to say."

No one had ever called my father a hero before, but now this single van driver in a foreign country of a billion people, a driver who never knew Dad, had called him one. In the airport on the last night of my trip, the tears finally came—not from all I had seen and experienced in India and China or from what I had learned about the Hump and Dad but from a Chinese man's heartfelt acknowledgment of my father's part in the war.

I still can't think of that conversation in the van without tears. Jack was right. Dad had done his duty despite dangerous flying conditions, fatigue, enemy fire, foreign surroundings, frightening weather, simple living con-ditions, lonely nights, tedious food and basic planes. That is a description of a hero. Then he returned home to do his duty as a husband, father and provider. He just died too soon.

But Dad is now out of a closed memory box, thanks to all the stories and observations that reflect who he was. And by reading backwards over the last several years, I have recovered more than details about Dad's life and more than my reawakened memories. I have gained a father whose patience, energy and curiosity shaped me more than I ever realized and who now accompanies me every day of my life.

The frustration and sadness of not really knowing Dad as an adult will always be there, as will my regret for not having pursued this information sooner. But I could only discover what I could, follow him where possible and, now, try to do better with my children and grandchildren.

Our history is to be shared, a hard-earned lesson. I accept with wistfulness that what I have learned about Dad and what I remember about him is enough for now, although I will never stop reaching out for more of his stories. I know they are out there, waiting patiently to be discovered, parts of his spirit just out of sight.

APPENDIX: THE JOURNEY CONTINUES

THIRTY-ONE

I Thought I Was Done...

*"Movies were outdoors. Sometimes we could hardly see the screen
through the rain. If we liked a particular scene (usually Lauren Bacall),
we'd have the operator play it over three or four times."*

—December 21, 1991 letter from a
Hump pilot to his son, Ken Ruzich

* * *

AFTER RETURNING FROM India and China, I expected to let the
trip's adventures settle in, recount our tales to friends and family, and
later write about it. But it wasn't long before opportunities arose to explore
new Hump connections. I continued to find more stories about life during
the war in India. Dad's experiences were still enriching my life.

Mack was talking about our trip to a friend in Davis, California. The
friend's father had also flown the Hump in 1945, the same year our father
did. They were both astonished to discover the connection. Ken's father
had had the foresight to write a wonderful letter to his children in 1991
detailing his time in India, which he shared with Mack. An excerpt from
that letter opens this chapter. My father could have written much the
same letter, with its description of trying to find Ascension Island in the
middle of the Atlantic, living in bamboo and grass baches, flying at twenty-
two thousand feet in every kind of weather, jettisoning leaking gasoline

barrels into the jungle below, and eating cans and cans of Spam—details that were now familiar to me.

A close high school friend told me that his father had been in India at the very end of the war and that he'd had to fly the Hump two or three times. His father had said that it was the scariest thing he had ever done. I told Bob that Dad had flown 150 Hump missions. His jaw dropped, and I smiled with pleasure and pride.

Even after the trip, I discovered that as the child of a Hump pilot, I had inherited the respect accorded my father and that it gave me an opening to talk with others, a passed-down connection. Dad was in a special fraternity and I enjoyed the legacy. If a friend learned of my quest to track Dad's footsteps and knew of the Hump operation, the response was always a nod of respect and an acknowledgment of the dangers of that posting. I assumed that I was too late to get to talk to any real Hump veterans (it turned out that I was wrong), but I heard stories from their children. Real World War II aficionados always jumped in with statistics of the Burma Road, the Flying Tigers and the Hump. They also wanted to know details about Dad. What plane did he fly? Where was he stationed? When did he serve? Before this quest, I had very little to contribute. Not anymore.

Three post-trip experiences stand out. I had unexpected opportunities to interview two living Hump pilots, thanks to my continued quest to discover more details of the operation. And I tracked down the daughter of Mont Jennings, the man whose interview had started this quest.

THIRTY-TWO

Hump Pilot John Stallings: January 2017

We arrive early at a restaurant recently opened in Dallas's NorthPark Center mall. I note with relief the carpet on the floor and the quiet booths. These will help us hear each other, a requirement I've only just begun to need as I've aged. I'm meeting John Stallings, a World War II pilot who flew the Hump. A friend, Sam Hocker, is bringing John to the restaurant. Sam and I serve together on a foundation board and always visit during our meetings. As a World War II buff, he was interested in my visit to India and China and volunteered that he had a friend who had flown the Hump, even offering to arrange a lunch and promising that John was still "with it."

I check the phone often for the time, anxiously glancing at the door. They are late. I hope he's not sick or, worse, has died. I don't usually jump to the worst-case scenario when a lunch date is tardy, but since John Stallings is ninety-four, I am holding my breath, hoping to get this unexpected opportunity to connect with a real veteran with firsthand knowledge of the Hump. He holds precious information that could answer some of my many questions. What did it feel like in the cockpit? What did you talk about up there? How cumbersome was the oxygen mask? What was the food like? Were you scared? Did you get any R&R? How did you get back home to America?

I see Sam first and, finally, behind him is John Stallings, a tall, dignified elderly man, leaning slightly on a cane, carrying a large briefcase overflowing with books and papers, an aged contrast to the many pictures I have seen of young, dashing World War II pilots. They approach our table and we're introduced, John giving me a firm handshake and a big smile. I like him immediately and linger over his face, imagining my father aged in this man's wrinkles, glasses, stooped shoulders, thinning hair, hearing aid and faded voice. He was where Dad was. This is as close as I'm ever to get to interviewing Dad, and I'm excited.

* * *

I REALIZED SOON into my search that I would have little chance of talking to a World War II pilot who had flown the Hump. By the time I started my search, all survivors would have been in their nineties or older, many with cognitive dysfunction. In fact, the Hump Pilots Association had been disbanded years earlier because of the loss of so many members. Mont Jennings died in 2008, two weeks shy of ninety. Leighton Maggard, Dad's friend from Plainview, the one he ran into twice during the war, had also died years earlier. My uncles were all gone. The closest I could get were a few individuals whose fathers had flown the Hump, but those were rare. Books offered recollections by Hump pilots, but none could provide a live personal interchange that would give me the freedom to ask for more details. All this made the connection with John Stallings so special and unexpected.

Before we could even order, John launched into a description of where he had been based in India and where his squadron had flown supplies to the British army fighting to push the Japanese out of Burma. Once the British had been supplied, his unit was sent farther north to fly supplies into Kunming, just as Dad had done. He seemed eager to talk, likely having few opportunities to share his stories, especially with someone who hung on every detail. I loved hearing him reminisce about flying over the "Rockpile," using the nickname I had only read about and confirming its insider use. He described the first time he saw St. Elmo's fire, a common occurrence on those flights, when the electricity in the thunderstorms would wrap a static charge around a plane's propeller cones or wings. "The first time you see that, you want to go home to your mother," he laughed.

Just as with other Hump pilot recollections, he had his story of being thrown up and down thousands of feet by air currents. He was right there, back in the moment, as he told of trying mightily to control the plane by thrusting up or down with full throttle, pilot and copilot both working to prevent the plane from turning over, and hoping to avoid mountains. He described coming as close to twenty-nine feet from the ground before pulling the plane up, causing my stomach to lurch with him in the telling. It was exciting to listen to.

He confirmed the availability of two ounces of whiskey after each mission flown. When he was flying into Burma, they occasionally flew three missions a day, meaning that six ounces of whiskey was the reward. He told of the "three for you and three for me" informal rule, as he always shared his alcohol with his crew.

John also substantiated much of what I had read of what was brought into the cockpit: a parachute for a quick exit when the plane couldn't be controlled and a knife and pistol for surviving in the jungle below. John had brought his own cavalry sword that could "hold an edge" and had tried to bring his own gun. "I'm from Texas and I brought a .45 revolver," he said. He was disappointed that the service made him leave it behind in the US, so he had only the standard-issue pistol. "I was a goody, goody boy," he said. "I should have kept it, but I didn't."

We covered his trip over from the States to India, which took fourteen days, traveling six to eight hundred miles a day in a new C-46. At Ascension Island, they needed to refuel in the middle of the Atlantic Ocean. His incompetent navigator, who "wasn't worth shooting," took them 120 miles off-course of the island before getting a reading. This was serious, as the planes had a limited amount of fuel. I exclaimed that some planes were lost over the ocean because they couldn't find the island and ran out of gas. John laughed and nonchalantly noted that after he landed, he was taxiing back to the terminal when he ran out, missing a sure death by minutes. Such an experience would give me nightmares, but this veteran shrugged it off.

As John talked through our meal and for an hour after, I envisioned my father telling his stories with the same animation and detail. I knew he would have had them. Every pilot did. And I suspect that his stories wouldn't have been much different from John's or from those others I had read about. I wished Dad was there, sharing his common tales with John and with us.

I asked John about flying after the war, about whether he wanted to. To my surprise, he replied that he was never interested. He had been in Kunming when the war ended. His crew was offered the option of flying a "war weary" C-46 back to the States. None of his squadron wanted anything to do with being in the air again for that long. They chose instead to take a boat from Karachi to the US, weeks slower but without any fear of crashing from the air or missing an island.

Back in the States, John had pilot friends who continued to fly, but he never felt safe in smaller planes after flying a C-46. He said he didn't dislike flying but admitted that he was scared the whole time like everybody else. That would have included Dad, who had to have been in scary situations. When told of Dad's continued love affair with the plane, he said some guys were like that. And he said that if Dad had been a crop duster as I described, he must have been a very good pilot, a compliment I accepted with a smile.

From his overloaded briefcase, John pulled out books that included photos of his squadron's unit, photos that showed him as one more young, lean smiling pilot. He loaned me a book with photos from the Hump operation, and my husband shared pictures from his phone of the Hump monument in Kunming. John hadn't heard of the monument and was surprised that the Chinese had done anything to acknowledge US help. I promised to send him a transcript of our interview for posterity and he thanked me.

For two hours, we both got to be back in India and China, telling stories in a restaurant in Dallas, surrounded by people who were simply having lunch with a friend or colleague. Only at our table was World War II being relived, an opportunity that will soon be lost because of our aging veterans. Our lunch had been a surreal mix of past and present, brought together by my search and by a lucky conversation with Sam. As I left the restaurant and walked away from John and Sam, I felt grateful.

In 2020, I tried to contact John Stallings to tell him about the impending publication of this book and learned he had died just days earlier. I realized how fortunate I had been to spend time with him in 2017 and that the door to personal Hump stories remains precariously ajar, soon to be permanently closed with the deaths of the last of the Hump pilots.

THIRTY-THREE

Mont Jennings' Daughter, Montessa

"My father only started talking about the war as he got older. He laughed about one method to prevent falling asleep on the journeys across the mountains. He would light a cigarette. When it burned down to the end, it would wake him up. He also talked about how cold it was in the cockpit. One night he was flying, and it was freezing. He looked at the copilot who was sweating. Dad asked how he could be so hot, and the copilot said he was thinking about some really hot peppers he ate in New Mexico one time."

— Montessa Jennings Fiveash

* * *

AFTER I RETURNED from India and China, I decided it was time to find out what had happened to Mont Jennings, whose interview by my aunt had started this journey. His simple confirmation of Dad's location in the war had given me a concrete starting point from which all else flowed. Given all the internet tools available and that he had such a distinctive name, surely I could find him or his family.

The first search yielded a Mont L. Jennings, born July 30, 1917 and who died on July 16, 2008 in Buffalo, Texas. He was buried in the Dallas-Ft. Worth National Cemetery. The dates and burial place were appropriate for a World War II veteran, especially since he had been born the same year as my father.

A second search adding Buffalo, Texas to his name pulled up an obituary of Phyllis Jennings, whose husband, Mont, had predeceased her. She was survived by her children and one stepdaughter, Montessa Jennings Fiveash. From there it was an easy pivot to Facebook to search for Montessa. Less than a second later, Montessa Jennings Fiveash appeared on the screen, along with photos and a confirmation she had gone to Monterrey High School in Lubbock.

Just like that, the deed was done. I was certain I had found Mont Jennings' daughter. Using Facebook Messenger, I wrote Montessa, explaining who I was and why I wanted to talk to her. She happily agreed to talk and we set a time for a phone visit.

Montessa and I bonded immediately. Her mother had died when she was thirteen; my father when I was sixteen. Both dads had loved to fly and both continued to explore the skies after the war. Mont Jennings had been the official commercial pilot for the Dunlaps department store chain in Lubbock and for the Dunlap family. Like my family did, Montessa had many memories of traveling in small planes, including one journey through a large thunderstorm that tossed the plane around and caused a St. Elmo's fire effect around the cone. Montessa and her mother held hands and prayed as her father concentrated on getting them through. He never looked scared, which Montessa attributed to his World War II flying experience. I was reminded of my story of Dad taking off on the very short runway in the Idaho mountains.

Montessa couldn't believe that I had a transcript of an interview with her father about the war. She loved the stories of our visit to Misamari and Kunming. She shared more memories: Her father had been struck by the people of India and Burma—"not black as Negroid and hair not as kinky as Negroids," reminding me of my father's description of the dark complexion of the African people. These were the observations of men who were seeing the greater world for the first time.

I had one important question. Did she know when her father had been stationed in India? I had pieced together a timeline that I thought accurate, but I still wasn't sure exactly when Dad had arrived in or left India. To my dismay, she told me that some of her father's World War II memorabilia had been lost in a storm when a large tree fell through the roof of her home—yet another frustrating setback. However, Montessa had inherited her father's books and possibly some World War II information, all of which was up in her attic. This gave her a reason to finally look through the box. She promised to try to find information about his time flying the Hump. I promised to send a copy of our interview, which I did.

Unfortunately, despite several more attempts to contact her, I hadn't heard anything more from Montessa until I read of her sudden death on Facebook, posted by her daughter. I felt I had lost a friend with a shared past even though we had never met. I noticed in her obituary that she had been very proud of the fact that her father had flown the Hump, a pride I understood. I will miss the connection and the hope that she could fill more holes in Dad's story.

THIRTY-FOUR

Australian Hump Pilot
Stuart Arnold: April 2018

"Your e-mail is very interesting, and I am willing to meet and talk to you. I have the full day available tomorrow (Monday) and if you call me ASAP we could arrange a time. Best wishes, Arnold Stuart"

* * *

I WAS DAYS out of a long-planned trip to Australia with my friend Mary Grace West to visit a mutual friend, Carol Douglas. The itinerary had been set, the weather checked, my passport updated and my wardrobe selected when Ed asked, "Did anyone from Australia fly the Hump?"

It was a question I hadn't considered, and it wasn't one I was sure I wanted to pursue. This trip was to be about relaxing and visiting, so different from the India/China trip. But I couldn't resist a quick Google search for Australian pilots who flew the Hump.

A year-old *Inside Science* article by Joel Shurkin popped up about a World War II C-47 that had been flown into China to be part of a museum exhibit in Guilin. I already knew about this event, which had taken place shortly before our visit to Kunming. The flight navigator was from Australia, which is why it came up in my search. As I perused the article, I came across Stuart Arnold, a ninety-four-year-old Australian pilot who had flown the Hump and was quoted about his experience. And then I saw it: Stuart Arnold was in Brisbane, the very Australian city I was flying into!

What were the chances of that? An Australian pilot who had not only flown the Hump, but who was still alive and competent and who lived in Brisbane. I had to try to find him.

My Australian friend Carol had many contacts, including a brother who oversaw pilots for Qantas Airlines. A former RAF officer, he referred me to a website that had information about World War II pilots—including, as it turned out, Stuart Arnold. As usual, I felt intrusive as I followed this man's military life without his knowing about it. He seemed to have been a good pilot with positive recommendations: "A sound and reliable all-round officer and a capable pilot." Arnold's record showed a last-known postwar address in Brisbane and Carol, who has a great sense of fun and adventure, suggested that we go to his old neighborhood and ask around. You never know who might remember him, she said.

So, on a beautiful Sunday morning, Carol, Mary Grace and I began knocking on doors around Arnold's last known address at 21 Ridge Street. I took the lead: "Hello, I'm Mary Clark and I'm from the States. My father flew the Hump during World War II and I'm trying to locate a pilot, Stuart Arnold, who also flew the Hump. He used to live in this neighborhood, and I was wondering if you remember him or know where he might be."

The response was warm and engaging. No one knew Stuart Arnold, yet we heard some poignant stories about residents' fathers who had been in World War II and what they had done. One neighbor took us through her home to the backyard to ask her husband to introduce us to an elderly man who lived down the street and who might remember. We had to make our way to the backyard swimming pool of another neighbor who chatted with us as she cleaned the pool. There was a debate among neighbors about who had dementia and who didn't. At our final stop, a woman recalled an Arnold family that had lived in the neighborhood years before; but she had no idea where they were now. It was a dead end, yet a most enjoyable one.

Belatedly, I realized that I could simply try to contact Joel Shurkin, author of the Inside Science article, to request Arnold's information. Shurkin had a website and email address, and I quickly wrote him. But time was becoming an issue: I needed to talk to Arnold the following day, before we left Brisbane. Fortunately, Shurkin's website also included his phone number, and I had Ed call him in Baltimore. Not long after, I received a nice email from Shurkin with Arnold's email address. Quickly, I wrote Arnold, explaining my desire to interview a World War II Hump pilot and asking whether I could meet him the following day. Within two hours, he emailed back the short note I quote at the beginning of this chapter. Several things were notable about Stuart Arnold's email. The first was that I had found him at all. The second was that a now ninety-five-year-old man could navigate email so well and that he wrote a thoughtful, cogent reply. I was impressed and hopeful.

Carol was familiar with Arnold's neighborhood and dropped me off the next morning. Stuart met me in khaki shorts and a gray National Rugby League polo shirt, only a small knee brace suggesting his age. I was a bit nervous and particularly excited to be in the presence of a World War II pilot in a foreign country. Hump pilots are rare, especially one who is still competent and articulate. Stuart Arnold was both. We sat down at his kitchen table and I noticed a pile of books and papers. He was prepared for my visit.

What followed was an hour-long interview, taking us back to World War II days but from the slightly different viewpoint of an Australian, one of only eight who had flown the Hump.

Like my father, Stuart had wanted to fly since he was young. When he was five, planes from an airshow flew over Brisbane and Stuart happened to be under the flight path with his mother. He was intrigued, and when World War II broke out, he couldn't join up quickly enough, signing the papers the day he turned eighteen. His training began locally, but he finished in Canada. Since there were more pilots than needed for an English posting, Stuart was posted at the Dum Dum base in Calcutta, living with other pilots in a requisitioned mansion, complete with swimming pool—so different from my father's thrown-together thatch-roofed bache in the Assam Valley. Stuart started flying transports all over India and parts of Burma. Later in the war his commanding officer approached him about flying the Hump, letting him know that he couldn't be required to fly the assignment. Stuart said he was surprised because he thought that when he signed up, he would have to follow orders. The Australians, however, considered the Hump to be such a hazardous mission that pilots had to volunteer. You could not be ordered to the post. Seven others joined him on the new assignment.

Some of Stuart's stories were familiar, such as the need to fly around thunderstorms, trying to find landmarks or radio beacons when they were thrown off course by strong winds, taking off on loud steel-mesh runways, using the deicer at high altitudes, and the difficulty of constantly wearing oxygen masks. He told of one navigator who didn't want to wear his mask, but when the man began to make directional mistakes at high altitudes, Stuart forced him to put it on. Stuart also had to take cigarettes away from some Frenchmen who were smoking in the hold, even when gasoline fumes were evident from the cargo. We both shook our heads at that story.

My questions were specific:

- *What did you carry into the cockpit?* A knife, a gun (with six bullets in case you had to shoot an elephant) and a parachute.
- *What were you most worried about?* Avoiding thunderstorms; just getting there, because no two trips were the same.
- *Did you have to deal with icing?* Yes, inevitable if there was moisture at twenty thousand feet.
- *What was your route?* We flew to Chabua in the Assam Valley where we had a cup of American coffee and then flew into Kunming (following my father's route).
- *Did you have a copilot?* No, but I knew that the American planes always had a copilot.
- *How was the food in Kunming?* Good. They had chicken.

Stuart's voice was soft and there was a loud drone from a lawnmower outside. I hoped my recording would pick up all the details he was giving me. He offered me tea, but I couldn't risk taking the time as I knew Carol would be returning soon. And I had this ridiculous fear that Stuart would have a heart attack as we spoke, and that I would lose his voice.

He told one story of having his parachute checked out only to discover two blankets inside the packets instead of a chute. "Some bloke was taking the parachutes into Calcutta to sell, where they were made into shirts. They caught him." Stuart laughed at the notion of floating from his airplane holding onto the corners of a blanket, making light of what could have been a serious situation.

At the end of the war, he said, he transported prisoners of war from Burma and Hong Kong. The men from Hong Kong were in relatively good shape, but those who had suffered in Burma were emaciated and sick. Mostly, though, he transported the same barrels of gasoline that my father had and at the same time. "Nineteen forty-five was a busy time over the Hump," Stuart noted.

What was different about the interview with Stuart was his postwar experience. Stuart continued to fly, but as a commercial pilot, and he put in seven thousand hours flying DC-3s with Trans Australian Airlines. The C-47 in the US Army, the Dakota in the Royal Air Force and the commercial DC-3 were pretty much the same plane, one described by Stuart as "the most reliable aircraft ever made." Because of his experience flying the military version over the Hump, the airline quickly hired him after the war.

"Flies like a dream," he said of the DC-3. "I fell in love with it." I told him that that was the opening of one of my chapters in the book, that I never expected to fall in love with a plane, and he laughed in recognition. Stuart even had a metal model of the DC-3 in his home.

I discovered that if my father had lived, he could have joined the Hump Pilots Association, an American organization that Stuart was a part of. Dad could have received pilot wings from the Taiwanese Chinese Air Force and the Hump Air Transport medal from the People's Republic of China. Stuart was wearing those in a portrait of him that his son had painted. He had also been invited by the People's Republic of China to go to Kunming for the 1993 dedication of the Hump Monument, complete with plane fare and first-class accommodations. When I described how well we were received on our trip to Kunming, Stuart wasn't surprised. I would love to have seen my father recognized in that way.

The hour passed quickly. Stuart had written his own book about his experiences and had other books about the Hump, including one from China that was written in English and Mandarin. I leafed through them, always hoping that one would include a photo of Dad.

I felt such a strong connection to this spry ninety-five-year old Australian, as though we shared a past, even though it wasn't mine but my father's. It seemed perfectly normal for me to be visiting him in his home in Brisbane, linked together by that long-ago war experience.

When Carol and Mary Grace returned, they took a photo of Stuart and me in front of his portrait. I promised to send him a copy of the book when it was finished, and then we parted, Stuart saying I had to return someday so he could fix me a proper cup of tea and me wishing that I could.

With Australian Hump pilot Stuart Arnold in Brisbane, Australia. Portrait is of the pilot himself painted by his son.

Timeline for My Father's World War II Service, as Discovered through My Search

June 3, 1940 – Ray Charles Walker graduates with a Bachelor of Science in Agriculture and obtains his Civilian Pilot Training. *Texas Tech Office of the Registrar*

October 16, 1940 – Dad, age 23, registers for the draft. *Dad's draft card, saved by my mother*

May 12, 1942 – Flight Instructor at Uvalde, Texas. *Student letter in my father's World War II trunk*

May 27, 1943 – Dad enters the service. *Dad's discharge summary, saved by my mother*

December 20, 1943 – Stationed at Love Field, Dallas. *Student letter in my father's World War II trunk*

March 1944 – Dad in Kansas City with the 33rd Ferrying Group. *Annual found in Dad's trunk and from reference in a letter from "Margie" sent to India*

Thanksgiving 1944 – Dad in Ghana. *Thanksgiving menu in my father's World War II trunk*

December 6, 1944 – Dad in Maiduguri, Nigeria. *Letter from Dad in Maiduguri to Gene Rutledge; shared by a cousin*

December 1944 – Dad in Maiduguri on a gazelle hunt. *Dated black-and-white photo; shared by my brother Gary*

Christmas 1944 – Dad in Maiduguri. *Christmas program in my father's World War II trunk*

1945 – Dad in Karachi, India. *Photo with Leighton Maggard, a friend from Plainview*

March 1945 – Dad in Misamari, India. *APO address on letter from "Margie"*

November 1945 – Dad back in the States and no longer flying. *War Department Officers' Pay, Allowance and Mileage Voucher, which wasn't burned with Dad's other war records and was available on request*

December 27, 1945 – Dad leaves the service. *Dad's discharge summary*

Served in Africa and Asia for 14 months. *Dad's discharge summary*

Flew 150 trips over the Hump between India and China. *Dad's discharge summary*

Bibliography

A HANDFUL OF historical books describing the Hump operation over the war, including some in Chinese, are available. A few articulate pilots have written memoirs of their time over the Himalayas. In reading some of them, I was struck by the common patterns in the experiences of the air crew. This helped me imagine Dad in the cockpit and what he had to manage on his flights. The difficulty of the mission appropriately supported the family myth chapter. But I still talk to people who are not familiar with the Hump and its significance. Far fewer books and stories have been written about this dangerous mission than the bigger operations in Europe and the Pacific. That is understandable, but it is an important story, hidden in the high Himalayas, that should be more widely read and appreciated.

Constein, Dr. Carl Frey. *The Hump: The First Airlift.* A personal memoir of a decorated WWII pilot with a concise history of the Hump.

Ethel, Jeff and Don Downie. *Flying the Hump*. Osciola, WI. Motorbooks International, 1995. Wonderful first-hand accounts by pilots of their experiences flying the Hump.

Plating, John D. *The Hump: America's Strategy for Keeping China in World War II*. College Station. Texas A&M University Press.

Shurkin, Joel. "Flying the Hump – 75 Years Later. When science and technology fail and only courage can win a battle." *Inside Science Magazine*, April 10, 2017.

Spencer, Otha. *Flying the Hump: Memories of an Air War*. College Station, Texas. Texas A&M University Press, 1992. Much of the information in "Flying the Hump: the Family Myth" (chapter 10) came from this excellent book. I found it on the internet and didn't realize until I received it that Professor Spencer had taught at what was then East Texas State University in Commerce, now Texas A&M University, just forty miles from where I live. It was another too-little-too-late, so-close-so-far experience, as Professor Spencer had died just a few years earlier, meaning I couldn't interview him. If I had started my journey earlier, I would have had a readily available resource.

Thomas, Nedda. *Hump Pilot, Defying Death Flying the Himalayas During World War II*. 2014. Palisades, New York. History Publishing Company.

Tuchman, Barbara. *Stillwell and the American Experience in China 1911-45*. 2017. New York. Random House.

Acknowledgments

I GRATEFULLY ACKNOWLEDGE the many who helped shepherd this quest to rediscover my father and to honor his WWII experience of flying the Hump. A posthumous thanks to my Aunt Helen Walker who had the foresight to interview Mont Jennings, the pilot who flew with my father. I wouldn't have known where to start without his words. My sister-in-law, Karen Walker, provided the initial encouragement and confidence to begin the journey. She also referred me to Mark David Gerson, an extraordinarily gifted writer/coach who helped bring into light the stories I remembered and those thought forgotten about my father. His creative comments and suggestions kept the book moving forward. I thank my extended family for their willingness to share their memories—my brothers, cousins, and my Aunt Winnie Moore, a major source for my father's past. To the friends who remembered often small details about Dad that helped illuminate his qualities, I am indebted. Though writings about the Hump operation are small compared to other WWII stories, I thank all those who wrote the books in my Appendix to educate me and others of this important slice of WWII history. And, finally, a particular recognition is needed for my husband who never wavered in his support of this project and always said, "Go for it."

About the Author

MARY WALKER CLARK is a retired attorney turned travel writer. Her essays may be found in the *Paris News*, at her blog, "Mary Clark, Traveler" and her podcasts at KETR, 88.9, an NPR affiliate. Clark is a contributor to the anthology *Still Me…After All These Years: 24 Writers Reflect on Aging"* and is an award-winning member of the North American Travel Journalists Association. Her independent approach to travel has reinforced an openness and acceptance of other cultures, a philosophy she shares in her writing. Clark is happiest when traveling a back road in a new country. She lives in Paris, Texas, and may be contacted at *maryclarktraveler@gmail.com*.

hellgatepress.com

Made in the USA
Monee, IL
23 December 2020

55454481R00125